Praise for *Let's Change the World*

"Having spent most of my professional life in an international organization, I wish I had the vision to write the book that Emiliana has written. In this book, she draws from decades of firsthand engagement with policymakers in developing countries and from rigorous research on those countries. There is much to learn from it, including reasons for genuine optimism about our capacity to help the world for the better."

—Elizabeth King, nonresident senior fellow at the Brookings Institution, and former Director for Education of the World Bank

"Emiliana Vegas is a Latin American trailblazer with profound knowledge and experience of the education sector. This inspiring book describes her successful career while navigating the complex world of international development. More inspiring, she provides lifelong lessons and advice that anyone can apply to excel at what they do best."

—Luis Alberto Moreno, former president of the Inter-American Development Bank (IDB)

"Emiliana Vegas has provided young professionals in the field of international education with a hugely valuable guide to managing their careers. Using touching and highly specific examples from her own background, she presents the main problems young professionals, particularly women and those from the developing world, are likely to encounter in large organizations. Her personal examples ring true, and I have heard the same from many other young or mid-career women. As an older male, who has been an official in such institutions, I wish I had had this guide myself, as a way of making such institutions more capable of using talented young women from the developing world."

—Luis Crouch, Emeritus Senior Economist at the International Development Group (IDG) of RTI International (RTI)

"The global organizations created in the wake of World War II to support educational development have contributed to considerable expansion and improvement. New challenges facing education systems call for even more effective, competent, and ethical global governance, and this will require attracting talented professionals to the field. Drawing on two decades of experience working for international development organizations, in many different countries and regions, Emiliana Vegas's *Let's Change the World* offers an engaging professional memoir and a roadmap abundant in professional reflections to a career in international education and development that will help those entering the field prepare for the technical, organizational, political, and ethical challenges ahead."

—Fernando M. Reimers, Ford Foundation Professor of the Practice of International Education and Director of the Global Education Innovation Initiative; Harvard Graduate School of Education

"I wish this book had existed when I began my career in international development! Vegas demystifies the range of international development organizations (from big employers like the World Bank to smaller, nongovernment organizations implementing programs). She provides detailed advice on how to get into international development work and—once there—how to thrive! She backs it all up with rich personal experiences. Vegas has worked in many of these organizations and advised many others. I'd recommend this volume to anyone seeking to enter the field."

—David Evans, Inter-American Development Bank

Let's Change the World

How to Work within International Development Organizations to Make a Difference

Emiliana Vegas

ROWMAN & LITTLEFIELD
Lanham • Boulder • New York • London

Published by Rowman & Littlefield
An imprint of The Rowman & Littlefield Publishing Group, Inc.
4501 Forbes Boulevard, Suite 200, Lanham, Maryland 20706
www.rowman.com

86-90 Paul Street, London EC2A 4NE, United Kingdom

British Library Cataloguing in Publication Information available

Library of Congress Cataloging-in-Publication Data available
ISBN 978-1-5381-9028-9 (cloth: alk. paper)
ISBN 978-1-5381-9029-6 (electronic)

∞™ The paper used in this publication meets the minimum requirements of American National Standard for Information Sciences—Permanence of Paper for Printed Library Materials, ANSI/NISO Z39.48-1992.

In memory of my parents,

Corina Vicentini and Luis Augusto Vegas-Benedetti,

who, with their unconditional love,

taught me the value of a great education

Contents

Acknowledgments

I am blessed and deeply grateful to have many individuals who inspired me throughout my education and career. Among them, the late Thaís Aguerrevere and Carmen Cecilia Mayz, my college professors who first showed me that a woman like me could also have a purposeful career and who were a source of guidance and support to me for many years after my graduation. Charlie Clotfelter and Helen (Sunny) Ladd introduced me to the field of economics of education and became mentors and friends. Luis Crouch and Gustavo Arcia helped me see how economics can be applied in practice to inform policymakers and introduced me to the world of IDOs; they too have been lifelong mentors and friends. Richard (Dick) Murnane, John Willett, and Caroline Hoxby believed in my potential and supported me through my doctoral studies. To date, there is no important decision I make without consulting Dick, and he and his wife Mary Jo have become family friends.

Nick Burnett, Beth King, Luis Alberto Moreno, the late Guillermo Perry, Juan Prawda, Lant Pritchett, and Eduardo Vélez-Bustillo opened doors for me in IDOs and mentored me along the way.

My sister, Maria Corina Vegas, has always been by my side through the good and bad, quietly (and sometimes loudly) providing me with love and support.

I could not have written this book without the initial support of my thoughtful son, Emilio Vicentini Abelmann, my friend and author Wendy Walker, and the author and "book doula" Rea Frey and her team at Writeway.

My former students Sarah Fry (HGSE '23) and Sooty Heng (HGSE '23) read draft chapters along the way and provided me with detailed feedback that substantively helped develop and refine the contents of the book. My thanks also go to Luis Crouch, Amanda Devercelli, Dick Murnane, and Eduardo Vélez-Bustillo for reading early drafts and providing helpful feedback. My Rowman & Littlefield editor, Michael Kerns, believed in the book before it even existed and helped me see it through to fruition.

Last but not least, my loving husband, W. David Lawson, and my two extraordinary sons, Emilio Vicentini Abelmann and Tobias Vegas Abelmann, provided constant love, support, and encouragement while I was writing the book (and as long as I've known them). Moreover, during the 2023 December holidays, they reviewed my draft manuscript and provided honest and helpful feedback. I am truly blessed to have these three wonderful men in my life.

Foreword

The title of this book is bold: *let's change the world.* It's a mission many of us are after. I've spent the last decade trying my best to do just that as a social entrepreneur, researcher, and as a part of international development organizations. Along the way, I've had the privilege of learning with and from many of the greats. In this book, Emiliana Vegas shows exactly why she is one of them.

A coffee date spawned this book. Emiliana and I met at Bluestone Lane Café in Harvard Square. I had approached Emiliana. We had "Zoomed" multiple times, had multiple mutual colleagues and friends, but had never had a proper sit-down in person. As someone who toggled between worlds—as the head of an academic center at the University of Oxford, an NGO leader, and working at the World Bank—I had found it hard to meet people who could connect the dots between these worlds. But Emiliana had traversed a similar path. She had spearheaded research projects, led departments at international development organizations (IDOs) like the Inter-American Development Bank (IDB) and World Bank, and sat on the board of private philanthropies like the Jacobs Foundation that directly funded implementation NGOs. I thought we would have a lot to talk about. And three hours later, the proof was in the pudding. Like this book, our conversation burst with insight and humor. I encouraged Emiliana to write a book about her experiences, and to my pleasant surprise, she did. I've come to appreciate that about Emiliana—she doesn't sit on ideas. She brings them to life.

In our conversation, I was struck by both Emiliana's substance and style. She shared small details which proved to be crucial bureaucratic lessons: how subtle differences in document names and format could lead to dramatically different approvals processes, facilitating faster translation between evidence and policy. Her stories struck a chord, navigating people politics and paperwork to achieve meaningful policy change. And at the end of our meeting, she kindly offered to drive me to my next destination in her sporty dark green car, windows down, laughing amid the Boston breeze. Throughout *Let's Change the World* I was similarly struck by both Emiliana's substance and style. I couldn't put the book down. The book covers must-know definitions, structures, and heuristics of IDOs, such as the "matrix," and then seamlessly transitions to a rendezvous with Shakira. And the book masterfully weaves together generalizable lessons with specific stories and vivid detail, crystallizing each point so the lessons land punchy and memorable.

Few books so gracefully combine the deeply personal with the constructively professional. In *Let's Change the World*, Emiliana shares openly about her high and lows—navigating raising a family as an ambitious career woman and coping with tragic loss. Consequential events closed some doors, and opened others, and Emiliana bravely shares which doors she marched on through.

In *Let's Change the World*, Emiliana shares key aspects of the incentives that govern influential institutions like the World Bank and IDB, from quotas on promotions and how to navigate them to striking the balance between increasing the size and spending of a loan made to the government—which is highly incentivized—and driving impact, core to the mission and motivation of many individuals in IDOs, yet often less incentivized than one might think. Another feature of IDOs is the ability to connect the dots between research and policy. Some IDOs are both global knowledge hubs and banks, investing in building schools, educational reforms, and more, yet the "knowledge" and "operational" aspects of these institutions can operate in silos. Connecting them is a mastercraft. In this book, Emiliana shares examples and lessons to better achieve the elusive goal of informing policy change with the best evidence available.

One of my favorite lessons in *Let's Change the World* is the importance of "getting your hands dirty." Sitting in a comfortable office, stewarding large loans and grants, and incentivized to engage in internal bureaucracy, it can be remarkably difficult to focus on the beneficiaries one is meant to serve. Emiliana reminds us how school visits can make all the difference. Not because an individual going to a school changes the world, but because caring about what happens in the school, and working relentlessly toward that, does. The emphasis on ensuring change happens on the ground, not just on high, resonated deeply for me. Emiliana encourages us to "travel to places where the final product of your work is located." I agree and would go a step further: those working in IDOs should work for implementation organizations too, grounding their work in experience on the front lines. This will maximize the chance of their high-level influence translating into classroom-level change.

On that coffee date, I was seeking Emiliana's advice. I had recently led an evaluation of distance-learning approaches during school closures caused by the COVID-19 pandemic. The pandemic had caused a historic disruption: over a billion children were forced out of school. An urgent question had gripped the global education community: how to provide education when school was out?

An NGO I had cofounded to scale evidence-based interventions, Youth Impact, tried a simple approach: tutoring via phone calls. Since over 80 percent of households worldwide have access to phones, this was a way to reach students at scale, even in low-resource contexts. In early 2020, we launched the world's first randomized controlled trial during the pandemic on distance education testing this approach. We started in Botswana. Schools closed in late March 2020; by mid-April we had launched the trial, and in mid-July we released the results. It worked. We disseminated the results far and wide. The global demand was extraordinary, and we soon started replicating the approach around the globe—in India, Kenya, Mexico, Nepal, El Salvador, Uganda, and the Philippines—with dozens of partners, including governments, NGOs, research organizations, and international development organizations, including the World Bank and the IDB. Again, the approach worked. We were stunned. And the program was remarkably cost-effective—for just $100, students had learned nearly the equivalent of up to four years of high-quality schooling.

Rarely do programs work, let alone across contexts and when delivered by governments. Equipped with an unusually robust evidence-base—some of the largest, fastest multicountry evidence ever generated in education—we asked ourselves "what next?" We felt ready to scale. And we wanted to build on budding partnerships with our partners, including the World Bank and the IDB. Who better to brainstorm with than Emiliana? Emiliana had worked at both institutions for decades, had headed up education departments, and was one of the rare individuals who could straddle worlds—both between research and policy, and between bureaucracy and impact. Having previously codeveloped the education pillar of the World Bank's flagship Human Capital Index, I had some familiarity with the inner workings of translating evidence to policy at an IDO. But I wanted to take things a step further. That day, and multiple times since, Emiliana shared ideas and insights which I have been grateful for and eagerly pursued.

In reading this book, I reflected more deeply on my experience working both in and with IDOs and their extraordinary potential to make the world a better place. And I learned even more than I thought I had from Emiliana already. This book is for everyone: those working with IDOs to know the ins and outs of how IDOs work, and those working in IDOs hoping to progress in their careers and, most importantly, to make a difference. Changing the world is hard, but equipped with some inspiration from this book, we just might make a dent.

Noam Angrist

Noam Angrist is the academic director of What Works Hub for Global Education at the University of Oxford and a cofounder of one of the largest NGOs dedicated to scaling-up evidence-based programs, Youth Impact. Noam has published in leading academic journals including Nature, Nature Human Behaviour, *and the* Journal of Economic Perspectives. *He has consulted for the World Bank Chief Economist and co-led the development of the World Bank Human Capital Index education pillar. He also led academic research underpinning flagship reports by the Global Education Evidence Advisory Panel, a structure co-convened by the World Bank, USAID, UNICEF, and the UK Foreign Commonwealth and Development Office (FCDO) which provides recommendations on cost-effective policies and interventions to improve learning outcomes in low- and middle-income countries. Noam was a Fulbright and Rhodes scholar and has a BS in mathematics and economics from MIT and a PhD from the University of Oxford.*

Key Life Events in Chronological Order

October 1, 1968	Born in Caracas, Venezuela
1975–1981	Jefferson Academy primary education and summer camp in Sargentville, Maine, USA
1981–1985	The Ethel Walker School, secondary education in Simsbury, Connecticut, USA
1985–1986	Independent studies to obtain equivalent high school degree in Caracas, Venezuela
1986–1991	Universidad Católica Andrés Bello, undergraduate education in Caracas, Venezuela
1991–1993	Graduate studies in public policy at Duke University in Durham, North Carolina, USA Summer 1992 internship, part-time job in 1992–1993 at Research Triangle Institute in Research Triangle Park, North Carolina, USA
July 1993–July 1995	Public policy analyst at Research Triangle Institute in Research Triangle Park, North Carolina, USA
August 1995–June 2001	Doctoral studies, Harvard Graduate School of Education in Cambridge, Massachusetts, USA
September 1998	Marriage to Charles H. Abelmann
March 22, 2001	Tobias Vegas Abelmann is born
September 2001–March 2003	Young Professional, the World Bank in Washington, DC, USA

January 20, 2003	Emilio Vicentini Abelmann is born
April 2003–August 2012	Economist (various positions), the World Bank in Washington, DC, USA.
September 2010	Divorce from Charles H. Abelmann
September 2012–July 2019	Chief of the Education Division, Inter-American Development Bank in Washington, DC, USA
July 2017	Marriage to W. David Lawson, IV
August 2019–March 2022	Co-director, Center for Universal Education, the Brookings Institution in Washington, DC, USA
July 2022–present	Professor of Practice, Harvard Graduate School of Education in Cambridge, Massachusetts, USA

List of Tables and Figures

Tables

Figures

List of Acronyms and Abbreviations

Abbreviation	Definition
AAA	analytical and advisory activities
ADB	Asian Development Bank
AFD	Agence Française de Développement (French Development Agency)
AFDB	African Development Bank
AIR	American Institutes for Research
ALAS	América Latina en Acción Solidaria (Latin America in Solidarity Action)
AM	aide-mémoire (memory aid)
ANEP	Administración Nacional de Educación Pública (National Administration of Public Education)
ASEAN	Association of Southeast Asian Nations
AU	African Union
BCG	Boston Consulting Group
BMGF	Bill and Melinda Gates Foundation
CariBank	Caribbean Development Bank
CARICOM	Caribbean Community
CGD	Center for Global Development
CIDA	Canadian International Development Agency
CN	concept note

CUE	Brookings Institution's Center for Universal Education
DECRG	World Bank's Group Development Economics Research Group
EAP	East Asia and the Pacific
ECA	Europe and Central Asia
ESA	Eastern and Southern Africa
ESW	economic and sector work
EVP	executive vice president
GIZ	Deutsche Gesellschaft für Internationale Zusammenarbeit (German Agency for International Cooperation)
GPE	Global Partnership for Education
HD	Human Development
HGSE	Harvard Graduate School of Education
HR	human resources
IBRF	International Bank for Reconstruction and Development
ICSID	International Centre for the Settlement of Investment Disputes
IDA	International Development Association
IDB	Inter-American Development Bank
IDO	international development organization
IEFG	International Education Funders Group
IEG	Independent Evaluation Group
IES	Institute for Education Statistics
IFC	International Finance Corporation
IIEP	International Institute for Education Planning
IMF	International Monetary Fund
IsDB	Islamic Development Bank
JF	Jacobs Foundation

JICA	Japan International Cooperation Agency
LA	loan agreement
LAC	Latin America and the Caribbean
LF	LEGO Foundation
LMICs	low- and middle-income countries
MC	World Bank Group Main Complex
MENA	Middle East and North Africa
MIT	Massachusetts Institute of Technology
MPP	master's in public policy
NGO	nongovernmental organization
Norad	Norwegian Agency for Development Cooperation
OAS	Organization of American States
OECD	Organisation for Economic Co-operation and Development
OEI	Organization of Ibero-American States for Education, Science and Culture
OPCS	Operations Policy and Country Services
OVE	Inter-American Development Bank's Office of Oversight and Evaluation
PCN	project concept note
PCR	project completion report
PER	project evaluation report
PISA	Programme for International Student Assessment
PIU	Project Implementation Unit
R4D	Results for Development
READ	UNICEF Innocenti's Research on Education And Development
RTI	Research Triangle Institute
SABER	World Bank's Systems Approach to Better Education Results
SDC	Swiss Agency for Development and Cooperation

Sida	Swedish International Development Cooperation Agency
SPD	Office of Strategic Planning and Development Effectiveness
SUMMA	Laboratory of Education Research and Innovation for Latin America and the Caribbean
TA	technical assistance
TL	team leader
UCAB	Universidad Católica Andrés Bello (Andrés Bello Catholic University)
UN	United Nations
UNICEF	United Nations Children's Fund (previously United Nations International Children's Emergency Fund)
UNESCO	United Nations Educational, Scientific and Cultural Organization
USAID	U.S. Agency for International Development
WB	World Bank
WBG	World Bank Group
WCA	Western and Central Africa
YP	Young Professional (in the World Bank Group's Young Professionals Program)
YPP	World Bank Group's Young Professionals Program

Introduction

I woke up at dawn to review and rehearse, one more time, my presentation. My twenty-year-old son, Emilio, was still sleeping in our shared hotel bedroom, so I stepped out to the small living room to avoid waking him up too early. Through the window above the desk, I could see our street in downtown Rome beginning to also wake up, with a few cars and small trucks parked to stock bakeries, cafes, and bars. In a few hours, we'd be in the Vatican, where Pope Francis was hosting a delegation of the Latin American Business Council—the owners of the largest industries in the region—to discuss how to increase cooperation to have more social impact. I had been invited to give a keynote speech on how to transform education in Latin America through improved private investment. It was June 2023, and I thought to myself, "How did I get here?"

My first full-time job, right after graduating with a master's in public policy from Duke University in 1993, was as a policy analyst at Research Triangle Institute's Center for International Development—now RTI International. It was there that I first learned about international development organizations. The scope of the work included travel to exotic places like Ecuador, Ethiopia, Tunisia, and Tanzania. The work as a policy analyst entailed analyzing data using statistical analysis packages and producing reports and presentations. I found it super interesting, a perfect combination of new challenges and, thanks to guidance from my supervisor, lots of exciting opportunities to learn and gradually develop new skills.

Then one day as I was on the phone with my dad, who was in my home city of Caracas, I said, "Well, work is not so great right now." I don't recall exactly what specific task I was complaining about, but I clearly remember my father's reply: "Well, Emiliana, if work was always exciting and fun, then why do you get paid to work?"

I was taken aback by my dad's curt response, hoping for a bit more empathy to lift my mood. I get that work is not always fun and exciting, but my limited professional experience had proven that work *can be* interesting, challenging, and rewarding. I wanted a career in which most of my working time would allow me to feel this kind of satisfaction. Gratefully, I have achieved this goal. How I got there is part of what this book is about. From my early professional years at the World Bank, where I had the opportunity to work different jobs within the same organization, to the Inter-American Development Bank as lead of its Education Division, I developed a broad overview of the role of development organizations and their role in policy impact. Seven years later, I jumped at the opportunity to become co-director of the Center for Universal Education at the Brookings Institution, a leading think tank, to help philanthropic organizations impact change around the world. When Harvard invited me to come back to the school as a professor, I couldn't resist the opportunity to pass along my experience to the next generation of leaders.

I passionately believe in the power of education to change lives and feel privileged to have been able to devote my career to this cause. I have spent my career working to bring evidence to inform education policy in the so-called Global South, particularly in Latin America and the Caribbean. My heart lies in bringing evidence to the hands of decision-makers, especially those working to improve educational opportunities for children in low- and middle-income countries (LMICs).

Most of my peers have pretty much had long careers in one sector and institution, for example, academia or a leading international development organization. In contrast, I have managed to have interesting, challenging, and exciting positions across think tanks, development banks, and academia. I blame my evolving career and array of experiences on curiosity and a desire for impact and job satisfaction. As a rule of thumb, when a specific job brings me a sense of purpose and excitement (and thus satisfaction) for at least 70 percent of the time, I stay. Once this share falls, it is time to move on.

Recently, I met up with Noam Angrist, who had worked in a few different types of roles—research, policy, and practice—and was on a mission to connect the dots between all three, with good evidence translating into real-world change. We met in a cafe in Harvard Square. Noam wanted advice on how to maximize ongoing engagements with two multilateral organizations, which seemed on the cusp of translating some exciting new evidence into large-scale change. I had spent most of my career at those two institutions, the World Bank and the Inter-American Development Bank, and I was more than happy to provide my perspectives to him.

We met at 3:00 p.m. at the Bluestone Lane Café. He laid out an agenda and topics of conversation, and I quickly realized this was going to be a longer-than-expected meeting. And it was. We talked past 6:00 p.m. (when I had to go catch the shuttle back to my apartment), and right before parting ways, Noam said, "You ought to write a book about your experiences." He continued, "Had we chatted ten years ago, it would have made navigating the ins and outs of these organizations much easier! And now that you're a Harvard professor, you can say whatever you want."

This has become my goal.

I feel very fortunate for the opportunities I have had to carve out a fulfilling career, and I am especially grateful to the many individuals who have given me advice and opportunities to grow. Just recently, one of them, Lant Pritchett, sent me a touching message. He wrote, "It is refreshing to see in your career trajectory that, over the long run, the whole 'nice guys/gals finish last' isn't true as you have always been nice and, while there have been some rough times, you have been at the top of the global education movement for a long time now."

He was right that there have been some rough times. Yet I have become a better, stronger person and learned valuable lessons because of them.

This book contains my reflections and lessons learned from over twenty years of working in international development organizations. My goal is to share with talented individuals who want to improve the lives of the most vulnerable populations in the poorest parts of the world. In my experience, global institutions have the capacity to dramatically improve opportunities for people living in LMICs. Yet, I also know that these institutions can be riddled with limitations and inefficiencies and that sometimes their staff are more interested in pursuing individual agendas than the institutional mission.

Luckily, I've lived through it all. I know there *are* people who really care in this field, and there *are* ways to operate on the inside that genuinely put the cause first and amplify impact. I want young people and professionals to know they *can* make a difference in the world by working within these organizations, benefiting from their resources, and dodging—or redefining—systemic setbacks and misaligned political agendas.

I hope this book will encourage those interested in pursuing careers in development to really *go for it*. With the right guidance and education, you can contribute to real and meaningful change in our complex world. And the World Bank, the United Nations, the Inter-American Development Bank, and similar international organizations provide a remarkable platform to do just that.

In this book, I share how to become a valuable member of these organizations, how to navigate them effectively, and how to make a *real* difference. The book is organized into three parts; in each I provide practical information combined with anecdotes from my own professional and personal journey. Part I: How You Get In describes the basic types of international development organizations, the kinds of jobs that are available within them, what the work is all about, and what skills you need to get in. Part II: How You Thrive is a deep dive into how to navigate international development organizations, including how to access internal resources to do great work, how to be both a team player and a team leader, and how to move up the corporate ladder. Finally, Part III: How to Make a Real Difference outlines how to identify the best people to work with (and for), how to build and develop effective teams, and how to balance having a fulfilling career with family. My goal is to help you find ways to have a purposeful career that makes a difference in the world, while also managing to have a loving family to come home to.

Together, let's change the world.

Part I

How You Get In

I

The Basics of IDOs

It was 1999. I was a newlywed, approaching the completion of my doctoral degree. My then-husband, Charlie, whom I had met at Harvard, had joined the World Bank (WB) in the Young Professionals Program (YPP) in the fall of 1997. Although I was primarily interested in landing a tenure-track position at a US-based university, I decided to apply to the WB's YPP. This was my backup plan in case I was not successful in the "job market," the period when higher education institutions post new faculty openings for soon-to-graduate doctoral students, postdoctoral appointees (postdocs), and nontenured faculty.

In early December, right before leaving our new home in Washington, DC, to spend the holidays at my parents' home in Caracas, Venezuela, I received the news that I had been selected for the final round of interviews for the YPP at the WB. My interview was scheduled for January 10, 2000, at the Bank's headquarters. My mother had recently died, and I would have liked to spend more time at home in Venezuela with my family. However, I returned to my American home in early January 2000 to attend the interview.

It was a very cold winter morning as I walked from our home in the Foggy Bottom neighborhood of Washington, DC, to the WB's headquarters for the interview. Under my long maroon wool coat (a hand-me-down from my mom), I was wearing a black skirt suit and a white blouse (in Venezuela, it is tradition to dress in all black for at least a month after a close family member's death). After making my way through the World Bank's security, an assistant met me to guide me to the room, where a receptionist behind a large desk took my name. In the chairs across from her desk sat the other competing candidates. We would all soon complete degrees in economics of education or development economics. We all knew of each other, having read some of each other's research and participated in the same conferences. At least three of us focused on education policy in Latin America. The Bank brought us all in on the same day for these interviews, but only one or two of us would be selected to the YPP. Needless to say, it was a stressful process.

A few months later, I was thrilled to get the news that I had been accepted into the YPP. It was a great backup option as I tested the academic job market.

But before moving on to the "real world" of work, I needed to complete my "job market paper," the key research paper in a dissertation. For the rest of 2000, I focused almost exclusively on making substantial progress on my dissertation research. I was also turning thirty-two in October, and the maternity clock was ticking. So, I decided to pursue both—finish the dissertation and (try to) have a baby.

I made progress on both fronts. I produced two research papers—a comparative study of teacher conditions across Latin America and an analysis of the relationship between teacher characteristics and student outcomes in Chile—and got a positive pregnancy test. I was ecstatic to know that I would soon be a mother!

Pregnancy turned out to be hugely helpful in completing my dissertation, as I work best under the pressure of firm deadlines. As one of my former Duke professors, Bob Behn, would often say, "The best man-made invention after the fire is the deadline." A growing belly certainly provided a very concrete reminder of my deadlines.

My doctoral adviser, Richard (Dick) Murnane, was going to be on sabbatical during the 2000–2001 academic year, and he asked if I'd be willing to teach his course on Microeconomics: A Tool for Educators. I was honored, excited, and very nervous. And, while he would not be at the Harvard Graduate School of Education (HGSE) most of the time during the semester, in exchange for teaching his course, he offered to meet with me as often as needed to discuss the progress of my dissertation. This provided another type of deadline for me, and I worked hard to make significant progress each week and take advantage of being in Cambridge to teach and meet with Dick to get regular feedback.

Every Monday and Wednesday morning from September to December, I taught Dick's economics course at HGSE to about fifty-five master's and doctoral students. Given the large class size, we were assigned Askwith Hall, a large auditorium in the lobby of the Longfellow Hall building. Askwith has theater-style seating, a front stage with blackboards and screens one can use to project from a computer, and a wooden podium with the HGSE logo. It is where most public events with high-level speakers are held. It felt intimidating to share the same stage and lecture graduate students, some of whom were older than me. But Dick had suggested that I use all his notes and materials, so I felt at least confident that I had strong content. In retrospect, I feel bad for the students who took my course that year (please accept my sincere apologies if you're one of them); they missed out on having Dick as their professor. It was a certainly a valuable opportunity for me to deepen my knowledge on the economics of education (there's no better way to learn something than to have to teach it), and I thoroughly enjoyed interacting with the students.

I was lucky to have an easy pregnancy. I did not have any of the common symptoms of nausea in the first few months and instead loved feeling the baby growing inside me and, later, his movements. As soon as Charlie and I could find out, we learned we would be having a baby boy. We settled on the name Tobias, a family name from his side that I loved because, among other reasons, it is spelled the same way and is easy to pronounce in both English and Spanish.

On March 1 of 2001, I turned in my complete dissertation (after having defended it before Dick and the other members of my Dissertation Committee), and twenty-one days later, on March 22, I delivered Tobias, a beautiful, healthy baby.

In the meantime, I continued pursuing the academic job market, and I landed two offers for tenure-track positions at two prestigious graduate schools of education. While an academic position had been my goal, I could not see myself in either of the towns where these schools were based. One was in the Midwest, the other in upstate New York, both with very cold weather and predominantly North American populations. I was not sure that I'd be able to find too many colleagues or friends with a similar background to mine.

After living in the vibrantly international areas of Cambridge and Washington, DC, the idea of moving to "middle America" was, frankly, unattractive to us. All of a sudden, joining the WB as a Young Professional became my best option. We were already enjoying life in DC, and I could start in the WB's research department, focus on publishing in academic journals, and in a few years transfer to a university in DC or nearby. I still had my sights on an academic career, but I would soon learn that staying open to great job options that allow you to make a difference is key to having a fulfilling career.

While I was born in a so-called developing country, during the 1970s and 1980s, Venezuela had a thriving economy and peaceful democratic transitions of government, and organizations like the WB or the Inter-American Development Bank (IDB) were not very visible. It was not until I came to the US for graduate school that I was exposed to international development organizations.

You too may be wondering, what exactly *are* international development organizations (IDOs)? Broadly speaking, they are institutions created to support development in low- and middle-income countries (LMICs), usually by providing resources (not only financial) to help them prosper.

There are many types of IDOs, which I describe in more detail later. To make it simple, I group them into five categories based on their primary role (see Table 1):

1. global funders (includes multilateral and regional development banks and bilateral agencies),
2. private philanthropies,
3. conveners/agenda setters,
4. advisers, and
5. implementers.

Table 1: Categories of IDOs and Selected Examples

IDO Category/ Reach	*Global Funders*	*Private Philanthropies*	*Conveners/ Agenda Setters*	*Advisers*	*Implementers*
Multilateral	IFC, IMF, WB	BMGF, JF, LF	Brookings, CGD, GPE, OECD, UN, UNESCO, WEF	AIR, Bain & Co., BCG, McKinsey & Co., R4D, RTI	Room to Read, Save the Children, UNICEF, World Vision
Regional	ADB, AFDB, CariBank, IDB, IsDB	Mastercard Foundation, Tinker Foundation	ASEAN, AU, CARICOM, OAS, OEI	Inter-American Dialogue, SUMMA	*
Bilateral	AFD, CIDA, FCDO, GIZ, Norad, Sida, USAID	*	*	*	*

* TOO MANY TO LIST

While I classify the main IDOs across these five types for simplification purposes, in practice most IDOs carry out multiple functions. For example, while I was working at the WB and IDB (examples of the global funders), I conducted applied research, convened meetings with government officials, and, of course, oversaw the banks' loans and technical assistance projects. While staff in IDOs do various types of activities, it is useful to identify the main function of each IDO. For example, there are important differences between IDOs that are *funders* (such as development banks and philanthropic foundations) and those that *convene*, *advise*, and/or *implement* programs funded by the international community (but do not themselves provide loans or grants to countries). As you can imagine, when you work for a funder organization, your primary responsibility is to provide financial resources (through grants and/

or loans) to recipient governmental and/or nongovernmental organizations but also, in many cases, technical assistance and advisory services. In contrast, when you work for non-funder organizations, you (or your superiors) are tasked with securing the financial resources to fulfill the organization's mission.

There are also important differences in the skills necessary to succeed in the various types of IDOs. For example, when I joined the Brookings Institution as co-director of the Center for Universal Education (CUE) in August of 2019, I was excited about transitioning from the unpredictable life of being division chief at the IDB, where I was constantly traveling, at times with only a moment's notice, to a premier think tank. I sought to make an impact through the Brookings platform and its core values of "Quality, Independence, and Impact." I was excited to focus less on management and more on applied research.

Before joining Brookings, I did not need to fundraise from external partners to conduct my work. Like most organizations that convene, advise, and/or implement programs funded by others, as senior fellow and co-director of Brookings' CUE, external fundraising would become an important part of my role. I also thought it was an important skill to develop, so I jumped right in. After a few months on the job, I learned how to connect with potential donors, find alignment between my own research interests and theirs, and write grant proposals and prepare donor reports. These skills are critical for succeeding in organizations that rely on external funding, like Brookings and many other nongovernmental organizations (NGOs). And many great career options involve fundraising.

Just as I was becoming more effective at winning over funders to support our work, I realized that I did not enjoy the added pressure of having to raise funds from external donors for practically everything. Brookings calls this the "footprint," which includes your (as a scholar) and your team's salaries and benefits, offices, technology, and administrative support.

As it turns out, unlike development banks that have ample funding thanks to the generosity of wealthy countries, the endowments that institutions such as Brookings have usually only covers a small share of operating expenses. While these institutions differ in how they fundraise, a significant effort to raise the necessary funds for maintaining personnel and operations is also required. While I was at Brookings, this effort was decentralized to each scholar, and those who were unsuccessful in raising their full footprint had to reduce their working hours or, in extreme cases, leave the institution.

Furthermore, I also realized that I am at my best when working closely with others toward a shared vision as opposed to being part of a group where every member works on their separate projects. While I valued the freedom that scholars at Brookings (and other independent organizations) enjoy, I missed feeling part of a team and the day-to-day interactions that come from working closely with others under tight timetables. After a little under two years with Brookings, I concluded that my role was not a great fit given my career aspirations and preferences. I applied my own rule of thumb and concluded that I was enjoying less than 30 percent of my time at work, and I decided to move on.

While you may not know yet what kinds of jobs are available, or the skills currently in demand that are the best fit for you, the sooner you understand the key differences among IDOs, the better prepared you'll be to secure the type of role wherein you will personally thrive and have the most professional impact. Table 1 presents selected examples of IDOs in each category, which I describe below in more detail.

Global Funders

When I was a summer intern at the WB, my supervisor, Lant Pritchett, explained, "If you want to work in international development, there is no better place than the World Bank." I agree that to have a career in international development, it is wonderful to start at the WB, which is the largest multilateral development bank. But it is not the only great organization within which to launch your career in international development.

In the *global funder* category, besides the World Bank Group (WBG), which includes the World Bank itself and several other affiliated institutions,[1] there are the International Monetary Fund (IMF); regional development banks, such as the Asian Development Bank (ADB), the African Development Bank (AFDB), the Caribbean Development Bank

(CariBank), the Inter-American Development Bank (IDB), and the Islamic Development Bank (IsDB); and many others. Specific to the education sector, there is the Global Partnership for Education (GPE), which brings together most large funders, including international development banks and large international philanthropic organizations, representatives from the poorest countries, and civil society organizations to help low-income countries access funding at even cheaper rates than would be possible through development banks. These are all called *multilateral institutions* because they bring together multiple funders who share the institution's mandate. In chapter 5, "Navigating the Matrix," I offer a deeper dive into how most development banks are organized.

Within some multilateral institutions, there are affiliated organizations that share the overall mission of providing funding and technical assistance to support economic development in LMICs. However, they do so by providing loans to private sector institutions, as opposed to public ones. Perhaps the largest of these affiliated organizations is the WBG's International Finance Corporation. The Inter-American Development Bank has a similar agency, IDBInvest, which lends to private sector organizations in Latin America and the Caribbean. Interestingly, the IDB also includes IDBLab, a smaller institution that provides smaller funds to government and nongovernment organizations for the purpose of innovating and experimenting with novel development solutions. When these innovative projects prove effective, the IDB or IDBInvest can then justify providing greater funding to the public (IDB) or private (IDBInvest) sectors.

There are also *bilateral* organizations that are led by a single country. The U.S. Agency for International Development (USAID) is an example. As in the United States, most high-income countries—Canada (CIDA), Finland (FINNIDA), France (AFD), Germany (GIZ), Japan (JICA), Norway (Norad), Sweden (Sida), Switzerland (SDC), and the United Kingdom (FCDO), among others—have bilateral aid agencies that fund programs in LMICs, often in partnership with IDOs such as the WB and the IDB.

Multilateral, regional, and bilateral international development organizations provide financial resources to LMICs through two main mechanisms: (1) loans at much lower interest rates than regular private banks, and (2) grants, which the borrowing countries are not required to pay back. Much of the work of technical staff within these institutions goes into designing and supervising the implementation of projects financed through loans and grants.

Working in a multilateral, regional, or bilateral IDO comes with some weight. Sometimes, the client (borrowing country government) values the funding more than technical advice and will go to some lengths to get the loan without really changing policies or improving outcomes. This is especially true in low-income countries and fragile states, where often the financial needs are the greatest and the proportional share of external funding is higher than in middle-income countries. On the flip side, in some countries (especially middle-income) where the share of external funding is far outweighed by domestic budgets, it is the IDO's advice that is most valued.

Multilateral, regional, and bilateral IDOs carry out ongoing policy dialogue with the client country governments and work with them to design new projects, aligned to national priorities and reforms. Once approved, the funding flows to the national treasury of the client country, and then the project is implemented through government and, occasionally, nongovernment agencies. Implementation is almost always the responsibility of institutions in the client countries. However, because presumably both the IDO staff and the country counterparts care about the success of the projects, an important part of the work of staff involved in lending or assisting with technical operations goes beyond mere supervision and includes helping solve problems that arise during project implementation.

Indeed, multilateral, regional, and bilateral IDOs have specific policies in place that require regular site visits to the projects being implemented for closer firsthand supervision. These visits, termed "supervision missions," are tracked internally through various documents that staff are required to submit, including a mission statement prior to the project visit, the aide-mémoire (or "memory aid") that is signed by the project's team leader and the government counterpart at the conclusion of the mission, and the back-to-office report.

Private Philanthropies

There also are many philanthropic foundations, or *private philanthropies*, that provide grants to governments and NGOs to improve the lives of people living in LMICs. Among the most active in global education (though this also varies over time) are the Bill & Melinda Gates Foundation (BMGF), Echidna Giving (focused on girls' education), the Ford Foundation, the Jacobs Foundation (JF, where I currently serve on the Board of Directors), the LEGO Foundation (LF, focused on learning through play), the Open Society Foundation, and the Rockefeller Foundation. This is by no means a comprehensive list as there are many, many other philanthropies carrying out meaningful work in these countries.

Many international corporations have also created their own foundations and/or have corporate social responsibility departments that provide grants to development organizations. These corporations and/or the foundations they support then work directly with low- and middle-income country governments. Some examples include the foundations derived from companies such as Amazon, Cisco, Dell, Hewlett, Mastercard, Meta, Microsoft, and Walmart. While these organizations provide financial and sometimes technical resources, they do not supervise implementation in the same systematic way as do the multilateral, regional, and bilateral IDOs.

As you can see, just between global funders and private philanthropies, many organizations provide financial resources and technical advice to IDOs. Sometimes they duplicate efforts, and often they overlap. Thus, there are organizations, some of which I describe below, that have taken on the task of convening key stakeholders to jointly develop, cooperate, and sustain shared agendas.

Conveners/Agenda Setters

When I was co-director of Brookings' Center for Universal Education (between 2019 and 2022), we held quarterly donor meetings to bring together all major funders in global education to discuss shared challenges. During the COVID-19 pandemic, we also collaborated with the World Bank and held a series of Leadership Dialogues, wherein we brought together former heads of state from various countries as well as current and past education ministers to discuss political strategies to maintain funding for education in the midst of a global health emergency. The more prestigious a convening organization is, the higher level the participants it can attract.

During this time, I learned how important it is to carefully plan these events, not only curating the main discussion topics and the list of speakers and participants, but also drafting the "run of the show"—a detailed, minute-by-minute script of how the meeting would evolve. Much of the work in convener-type organizations is about selecting interesting topics and hosting public and private high-level events.

In the *conveners* category, the largest and arguably the most influential worldwide is the United Nations. The UN was founded in 1945, after World War II, to promote global cooperation to maintain peace and ensure the protection of human rights and global agreements. The UN works across various sectors, including education.[2] The UN Education, Science and Culture Organization (UNESCO) is the lead global convener of high-level government officials to pursue shared education goals. To work at the UNESCO headquarters (located in Paris, France), perhaps the most important skill is diplomacy. UNESCO professionals need to be able to persuade member nations' representatives to sign global agreements. These representatives from member nations are often former government officials, such as ministers and ambassadors. Although some technical knowledge is useful, to have an impactful career in UNESCO, diplomatic skills are the most advantageous. Some UN agencies implement programs, and I include them in the *implementers* category, discussed below.

The Organisation for Economic Co-operation and Development, or OECD, is often referred as "the wealthy nations' club" because it brings together high- and middle-high income countries to foster evidence-based cooperation. Within education, its international assessments, for example the Programme for International Student Assessment (PISA), have had a significant impact on low- and middle-income country education policies.

The Organization of Ibero-American States for Education, Science and Culture (OEI, where I currently serve on the Global Advisory

Council) brings together nineteen countries that share the Spanish and Portuguese languages to promote cooperation in education, science, technology, and culture.

At the regional level, there are organizations whose main mission is to promote cooperation and push forward shared agendas. The Organization of American States (OAS) defines itself as "the premier regional forum for political discussion, policy analysis and decision-making in Western Hemisphere affairs."[3] The African Union (AU) consists of fifty-five member states from the African continent whose mission is to increase cooperation and integration to drive that continent's economic development. The Association of Southeast Asian Nations (ASEAN) serves a similar role in that region. The Caribbean Community (CARICOM) groups twenty countries, most of them island nations, stretching from the Bahamas to Suriname and Guyana in South America, to promote regional cooperation.

There are also nonprofit IDOs, such as the Brookings Institution, the Aspen Institute, the Center for Global Development, the Inter-American Dialogue, the World Economic Forum, and many others, that play an important role in convening stakeholders and setting common global and regional agendas.

Additionally, in many sectors, there are "funders' groups," like the International Education Funders Group (IEFG), that bring together diverse funders to learn from and collaborate. These organizations vary in size, staff composition, and priorities, as well as amounts and sources of funding. They therefore recruit for different skills and offer different professional growth pathways for early and mid-career professionals. The larger the convening organization, the more likely it is to invest in professional development and establish pathways for individuals to advance internally. In contrast, smaller organizations can be valuable stepping stones, as they may sooner offer young professionals roles that have greater levels of responsibility, and thus greater exposure, as compared to larger organizations.

Advisers

When I was a young policy analyst at Research Triangle Institute (RTI) between 1993 and 1995, my boss, Luis Crouch, invited me to attend a high-level meeting in Washington, DC. RTI was a subcontractor, meaning that another organization had contracted with us, for a USAID-funded project. Luis had been the lead researcher for a report titled "Policy Dialogue and Reform in the Education Sector: Necessary Steps and Conditions," and he had generously included me. I had conducted some of the background research and initial drafting alongside the then–vice president of RTI, which I learned later is a politically savvy move common in all IDOs to include superiors as coauthors. The reason is that the majority of those in leadership positions at IDOs began their careers as technical staff, leading research and report-writing. Once they reach leadership positions, they often have little time to conduct research or write reports, yet they spend a great deal of time reviewing and approving them. Including them as coauthors does not cost much, and yet it signals that you value their contributions and may even give you some internal "brownie points."

At the meeting, in the USAID's offices in Washington, DC, Robert, a representative from the contractor firm, explained to the USAID official that he had thought of the initial idea for the report and then hired Luis and his team to put it together. My eyes popped! I knew firsthand that Luis had not only had the original idea, but had been the brain behind the substance of the report. Luis didn't blink, and the conversation continued without a hitch.

After the meeting, as we were waiting by the elevators, I turned to Luis and exclaimed, "Luis, I cannot believe what Robert just said during the meeting—that he hired you to implement *his* ideas. It was so insulting!" Luis replied, "Emiliana, I was not insulted. That is how some of these organizations work. Don't worry. Everyone in the room knows who *really* has the ideas and substantive contributions."

Luis was right. I found a wide variation in the quality of the advice from the kinds of organizations I refer to as *advisers*. These organizations provide technical advice and knowledge as well as primarily focus on strengthening the capacity of governments to deliver public services, as in the sectors of education and health. Although some of the funders and conveners described previously may also serve as advisers, the distinctive feature of the organizations I include in this group is that most of their work is for a client, be it a policymaker, a multilateral or bilateral development organization (like USAID), or a convening organization (like the Brookings Institution).

Funders and governments often seek out external technical advice from nonprofit research institutions like Research Triangle Institute, the American Institutes for Research (AIR), or Results for Development (R4D), as well as international consulting firms like Abt Associates and Mathematica. And, of course, funders and governments are also able to contract large international consulting firms like Bain & Co., Boston Consulting Group (BCG), and McKinsey & Co. to receive advice on their specific development and/or organizational challenges.

In the education space, there are several institutes affiliated with UNESCO that provide advice to policymakers across the world, including those within the International Institute for Education Planning (IIEP, where I currently serve on the Governing Board) and the Institute for Education Statistics (IES), headquartered in Toronto, Canada.

The organizations in the advisers group are a promising avenue if you want to explore working in a variety of development sectors and regions. They are a worthwhile option for recent college and master's graduates with limited work experience. Large international consulting firms are well known for their internal training programs for early career staff, and some of the larger international nonprofit organizations have ample training and professional development opportunities for early career professionals. To work within organizations in this category of IDO, the most important skills are the ability to effectively analyze complex problems and communicate clearly, especially in writing.

Implementers

In December 2009, the results of the Programme for International Student Assessment were released. My World Bank colleague, Harry Patrinos, and I had recently moved from the Latin America and the Caribbean Education team, where Harry and I had been leading the

Bank's operations (from its headquarters in Washington, DC) in Mexico and Chile respectively. One day Harry said to me, "Emiliana, you deserve a raise. Chile's scores were among the highest of Latin America." I replied, "Well, Harry, if that's the case, you will have to take a pay cut—Mexico did pretty badly." We both laughed because we understood that when you're working in an organization like the World Bank trying to affect a country's education policies, your work is very far removed from the actual beneficiary, in our case the students, and it takes time for policies to have impact on the ground.

I have never worked in an organization that primarily implements projects and programs. That said, I think *implementers* are some of the most exciting organizations to work for because you can sooner and more readily have a direct impact on the people whose lives you care about improving.

The UN Children's Fund (UNICEF) is the lead agency implementing education programs in the most marginalized areas of the world. UNICEF is headquartered in New York City and has offices in most low- and middle-income countries. It is primarily an organization that designs and implements education programs to serve the most marginalized children. UNICEF staff tend to spend a lot of time on building strong engagement and relationships with client country governments. Also, because they are not funders, it is primarily through those relationships that they can exert influence. They do more "project" work, rather than advising on major policy reforms like global funders. To work in UNICEF, it is helpful to have strong project management and operational capabilities.

Like UNESCO, UNICEF also has some affiliated institutes, including the UNICEF Office of Research–Innocenti (known as UNICEF-Innocenti), based in Florence, Italy. UNICEF-Innocenti conducts research on issues related to child and adolescent well-being, including issues related to education, child labor, and poverty. To work in this institute, you must be interested and skilled in social science research.

Numerous international NGOs implement programs funded by other IDOs. In the education sector, some of the most widely known include the Aga Khan Foundation, ChildFund International, Plan

International, Save the Children, World Vision, Room to Read, and Imagine Worldwide. Again, this is not at all a comprehensive list!

Categories and Types of Jobs within IDOs

Let's turn now to the kinds of jobs that exist within IDOs. For staff, there are two broad categories. First is the *technical* staff, who conduct research and analytical work as well as manage the direct lending and technical assistance programs within countries. The second category is the *support* staff, which includes procurement and financial managers as well as legal and human resource specialists. In addition to staff, there are *consultant* positions in both technical and support areas. My own experience, and therefore the focus of this book, is the technical category.

Within both the technical staff and support staff tracks, there are international staff positions and local staff positions—each with distinct working conditions, career opportunities, and financial benefits.

International staff positions are designed to offer a lifelong career within IDOs and are attractive, and thus competitive, because these positions include compensation packages that are appealing and competitive enough to attract professionals from all member countries—including wealthy countries like Denmark, Finland, and Sweden, whose national laws include generous benefits to their workers.

Local staff positions are based in IDO offices located in borrowing member countries and are aimed toward professionals who are citizens of those countries and can contribute relevant local knowledge as well as provide valuable continuity to these projects. Local staff are not subject to the rotation I describe below; however, they do have access to professional development opportunities. The compensation packages of local staff are designed to be competitive within each specific country, as opposed to in relation to the world in general. Therefore, while the pay and benefits are usually better than for comparable jobs within each specific country, they are substantially less than those of the World Bank's international staff.

Rotation

In most IDOs, international staff are expected to rotate to new jobs on a regular basis (anywhere from three to five years usually). This expectation for rotation brings benefits (opportunities to live in different parts of the world and work on new and exciting opportunities) and challenges (in particular for balancing family life, for example, if moving is required and impacts children and spouses). When I worked at the WB and the IDB, there was a 3-5-7 rule that applied to all international staff. It required international staff to remain in a specific unit for at least three, on average five, and at most seven years (though you could be promoted within the corporate ladder—more on this topic in chapter 10, "Moving Up the Corporate Ladder").

In recent years, however, the WB introduced a "batch" system, whereby all international staff are required to rotate every four years. The "batch match" or "batch rotation" occurs annually and staff who have been in a post for four years must enter. Through this process, staff have an opportunity to indicate their preferences from a list of available positions (and sometimes complete an interview). If a specific staff member does not find a "match," they can stay in the current post for one more year and must participate in the batch match the following year. After two failed rounds, they may be asked to exit the WB. This type of regular rotation exercise is commonly found in bilateral or civil service entities.

Because international staff typically move every four or five years across regions (whether in the actual countries and regions or working for them from headquarters in Washington, DC) and sometimes sectors, many IDOs provide professional development opportunities, especially for international staff. For example, as part of the YPP, I was able to receive individualized language instruction—I attempted to learn Portuguese, which was paradoxically very difficult for me because it is very similar to both Spanish and Italian. As a YP, I also benefited from a weeklong, off-site "Introduction to Team Leadership" professional development course at a beautiful resort in the state of Virginia. As I advanced through the ranks of the World Bank, I was selected to participate in their Corporate Leadership Program. This was a joint initiative between the WB and the International Finance Corporation—the organization within the World Bank Group that lends to private institutions in developing countries. The Corporate Leadership Program brought together promising emerging leaders who had the potential of one day becoming part of the WBG senior leadership team.

Beyond staff positions, all IDOs rely on consultants, which can be either international (if based in HQ or outside their own country of citizenship) or local. The key difference between staff and consultants is the length and strength of the employer-employee relationship. Consultant contracts tend to be short-term and do not have health insurance, paid vacation, maternity leave, contributions for retirement, etc. In the IDB and WB, there is also an "extended term consultant" which is a one- to four-year contract with no possibility for extension and some benefits (health insurance and paid vacation).

While these job types are distinct, in practice there is some fluidity and the right choice for you may change depending on family or other issues that influence your decisions. Some consultants become permanent and work for an IDO for years on a part- or full-time basis but without benefits. Some consultants try and succeed in becoming staff, and some local staff convert to international staff positions.

Now that you have a basic understanding of the main types of IDOs and job categories, I wish to offer some advice, which will differ in relevance depending on your career stage.

If you're a college student considering starting a career in international development, where should you try to get a job? To be honest, it will be almost impossible for you to get a position, even as a consultant, in the large development banks or the UN agencies. They almost always require graduate degrees.

It may be difficult, though not impossible, to secure a job in the IDOs that I have described as *advisers.* Large consulting firms, such as Bain & Co., BCG, and McKinsey & Co., recruit by cohorts, and they target top-performing students from highly selective colleges and universities who first enter as a summer intern, with the potential to be retained after their college graduation. These summer internships are highly selective, and if you are indeed interested in working for this type of IDO, it is best that you consider applying during your second year of college.

Nonprofit research institutions like RTI and R4D often hire college students as summer interns as well as soon after college graduation according to their project needs. Depending on your experience and skill set, you could be assigned to work in research, in project operations on the ground, or a combination of the two. These advisory research institutions are ideal organizations through which to get your feet wet in the world of international development.

Similarly, convening organizations, such as Brookings and the Center for Global Development (CGD), offer summer internships to college students and entry-level positions are available to recent college graduates. These organizations are a great fit for those who are interested in supporting researchers, either in the actual research or as part of the dissemination process, which often includes organizing high-level events. As a young professional, you will gain broad exposure to many different topics and high-level actors, such as former heads of state, current and former secretaries, and government ministers, as well as other thought leaders within international development and education.

One key distinction between international consulting firms and research-based institutions like Brookings and CGD is that the former recruits very selectively to invest in its recent graduates to grow within the organization. At Brookings, there was no path between early career (summer interns, research assistants, and other non-scholar) staff and becoming a fellow. In this case, the expectation for college graduates is to work for the organization for about three years and thereafter pursue a graduate degree to be eligible for the scholar jobs or altogether move to a different organization.

Are you a master's or doctoral student looking to launch a career in an international development organization, or are you a mid-career professional looking to shift toward international development? Depending on your academic and work experience, you could consider a full-time staff position or a consulting job in multilateral and bilateral IDOs, the UN agencies, and most of the other IDOs. But the key point is that the types of jobs for which you may be eligible will depend on your academic and work experience. My suggestion? Visit the job openings websites of these organizations to view their current vacancies, which explain the academic and work experience requirements. You'll likely find the contact information for someone within the organization that you could contact if you wish to inquire about the details of the listed position or clarify your understanding of the job description, which are often vague and copy-pasted from previous vacancies. Don't hesitate to reach out and ask.

2

The Skills You'll Need

Why do you want to get more schooling? You're already a professional!
—My dad, Luis Augusto Vegas-Benedetti

As the second child of four to two young Venezuelan parents, I had the benefit of a driven older sister, and parents that achieved financial success and who greatly valued education. Even though my mother had only finished high school and my father had been unable to graduate from college because he was summoned to work in the family business, throughout most of my childhood and teenage years, we were a privileged family.

Throughout the 1970s, 1980s, and mid-1990s, my father ran a successful family business and held leadership positions in several business-led organizations, including the Caracas Chamber of Commerce. He was also interested in public service and was appointed governor of Caracas by the president of Venezuela, a position he held for two years in the mid-1970s. Unfortunately, a confluence of factors—including my mother's cancer diagnosis and premature death as well as the presidential election of a communist-leaning, authoritarian leader during the last years of the 1990s—led to the loss of the family business and other family assets.

Some of my earliest memories include my parents sharing that they intended to send my siblings and me to boarding schools in the United States. They believed there were no excellent schools in Venezuela, and while this would be a significant investment and sacrifice for our family, it would indeed be worth it. From my very early childhood years, my parents instilled in me the notion that a high-quality education could be transformational.

When I was six, and my sister seven, my parents enrolled us in Jefferson Academy, a new private bilingual English-Spanish elementary school in Caracas. The tradition in our family and among friends had been for children to attend single-sex Catholic schools: my mother had attended San José de Tarbes, and my father San Ignacio de Loyola. Yet, feeling that it would limit our thinking, our parents turned away from Catholic education. They believed that Jefferson would give us a better foundation to learn English and to gain a more global and perhaps less dogmatic perspective of the world.

Back then, Jefferson Academy was a very small school with only three classrooms. It operated from a residential house in the middle-class neighborhood of San Román, about a twenty-five-minute car ride from our home. Half of the school day was spent in English class, where we learned to speak, read, and write in that language, and the other half in Spanish-medium lessons during which subjects such as math and social studies were taught. As word spread about the school, enrollment grew.

The truth is, while the infrastructure and facilities of Jefferson Academy were not up to par with those of other private schools in Caracas and other wealthier countries—for example, we had no playgrounds, sports facilities, or music rooms—we had arguably the best teachers in the country. Our English-language teachers were native speakers, which was not the case in other bilingual schools. I was taught to diagram sentences to learn English grammar during fourth grade by Miss Elizabeth—who managed to make learning English grammar fun! Plus, she was blonde and blue-eyed—a rarity in Venezuela. To me, she looked as beautiful as the Barbie dolls that I had seen on the American TV channels that we could access through satellite. My fifth-grade English teacher, Miss Dru Anne, had us participate in spelling bees, which I almost always won, except for when the final word was "rhythm," and my classmate Tony beat me.

Our small school was like a family. Miss Pedroso, the school founder, and her daughters all worked at the school, and our Spanish teachers in grades 3 through 6 were two sisters, Miss Miriam and Miss Fulvia. They were both warm and loving, and they always made us feel safe. Many years later, we now have a group chat on WhatsApp of which they are also active participants. On this group, one of my former classmates recently posted an old picture of Miss Fulvia with the tagline, "When we were happy and didn't know it."

Upon reflection, later in life, I have developed an enormous respect and admiration for quality teaching. I am an example of what those teachers were able to mold during those formative years.

As an extension of my parents' commitment to us becoming fluent in English, during our elementary school summers, from the young age of eight and seven respectively, my sister and I traveled over 2,300 miles to attend summer camp in Maine for a whole seven weeks! This became a tradition that continued, despite our protests, for another three years. The camp was *very* rustic. It was situated in the middle of the woods with access to a lake; there were a few wooden cabins to sleep in, a main cabin to eat in, and, to my distress, absolutely no showers. To bathe during the week, girls had the option to lather shampoo and soap in the lake on Wednesday afternoons.

On Sunday mornings, however, all sixty-odd girl campers were required to skinny-dip in the lake simultaneously with shampoo and soap. This was quite traumatic for my sister and me (the only non-US campers), as we had been raised to be very modest and protective of our bodies. After the first year, my parents finally got the message from our pleas and asked the camp management to exempt us from the skinny-dipping part of bathing. I don't know what was worse—taking off my clothes and bathing naked with another sixty girls, or to have the head of the camp announce to the other girls that some girls were just "different," because they came from other cultures, and thus we would be allowed to wear bathing suits from now on.

These long and faraway summer camps took place during the mid-1980s when there were no mobile phones or internet access. Over and above this, our camp had a strict policy of no phone calls between parents and campers during the seven weeks. We could only communicate with our family back home via "snail mail." And it was slow. *Very* slow. Yet, every weekend, we would write to our parents asking them to pick us up from camp early. I even wrote to my paternal grandmother, pleading with her to order her son to come pick us up from that awful place!

I also hated the mandatory 8:00 a.m. swimming lessons in the lake, which was freezing cold compared to what I was used to in the Caribbean seas. Not being able to shower, and feeling so much shorter, younger, and less fluent in English than everyone else in the camp, took its toll. But my parents would not relent, and we continued to go every summer for four years—until we started boarding school. I am convinced that, to this day, the notion of going camping terrifies me because of the summers I spent at the dreaded Camp Four Winds.

Of course, it is likely that because of this camp we became truly fluent in English, which helped my sister and me gain admission to an elite boarding school in New England, changing not only my education but, more broadly, my life trajectory.

In the fall of 1981, right before my thirteenth birthday, I followed my sister, who a year before attended the Ethel Walker School (Walker's), an all-girls boarding school in Connecticut. I can't say it was love at first sight. I was at least a year, often two, younger than my classmates. I was also (and still am) quite short. More importantly, I was very much a girl, as opposed to my preteen or teenager classmates. The posters of the rock group AC/DC that my roommate brought were quite a contrast to my poster of Holly Hobbie, a girl with a pastel-colored dress and bonnet.

Yet, it was at Walker's where I first became truly excited to challenge myself in new areas. I thrived in the small, discussion-based classes and quickly learned to self-manage my time. I decided to learn French as a third language. Although I had taken ballet lessons twice a week for at least four years at home, I was not selected for the elite "Dance Workshop" when I first auditioned. Later, after spending almost a year watching the Dance Workshop members rehearse four times per week, right before my own dance lessons, I was finally accepted in the spring of my freshman year. Being in the Dance Workshop was a significant time commitment, and the school considered it as credits for both sport and music. I had also been taking piano lessons back home, and at Walker's I continued more intensively. In addition, I invested my time in voice lessons, singing in the choir and the school's a cappella group, running for school government positions, and writing for the school newspaper.

Although I remained busy and challenged at boarding school, I also experienced extreme homesickness—missing my family, friends, the warm weather, and the food in Venezuela. The social scene of teenage girls in boarding school was very different from my social circle back home. At Walker's we had monthly dances with nearby all-boy boarding schools—sometimes at our school, but more often at theirs. I went only a handful of times as I was very shy, and being bused to a party where I knew none of the boys and the goal was to find somebody to "make out" with was not my idea of fun.

At home, my parents and their friends hosted parties for teenagers to meet each other practically every weekend, and I had always known at least some of the girls and boys. Plus, I didn't have to arrive by bus and thus be forced to stay until the very end of the event, even if I was not having a good time. Sometimes I was able to ask my parents or my friend's parents, who had been chaperoning the dance, to take me home earlier. It was during my vacations in Venezuela that I learned to dance salsa and merengue and to enjoy dancing with boys just for fun, without the social pressure of becoming more involved.

Though I ultimately graduated from Walker's cum laude and received several awards that would likely have contributed to my gaining acceptance to a top tertiary education institution in the United States, I was relieved that my parents supported my decision to return home to attend college in Venezuela. It is only now in retrospect that I consider the difference in tuition costs between American and Venezuelan universities to have played a significant role in their supporting my decision. My dad raised us to never discuss the financial matters of our family. Women were not supposed to know how much things cost, and as a result, I only began learning how to manage my own finances in adulthood—far later than I would now recommend.

Going back home for college meant that I had to make important career decisions early. In Venezuela, as in most of Europe and Latin America, and unlike in the United States, one does not apply to a university or college and thereafter declare a major. Instead, high school seniors apply to specific programs of study that are usually four to six years long. I was seventeen when I was required to choose the career I would pursue. I decided to apply to the five-year program in social communications at one of the best private universities in Venezuela, the Universidad Católica Andrés Bello (UCAB, Andrés Bello Catholic University). It offered a wide array of courses in history, literature, and the social sciences, and there were options to major in areas like journalism, audiovisual communications, or marketing. It was comparable to a liberal arts degree in a US-based college.

It was at UCAB that I first came head-to-head with the concept of inequality of educational opportunity. The social communications program was highly competitive. To be admitted, prospective students had to have a strong academic high school record as well as the highest scores in the centralized national university admissions test. Thus, my classmates were among the strongest students from across the country.

I soon realized, though, that I was one of the best prepared. While my peers often struggled to excel academically, sometimes just managing to pass a few of the courses, I achieved high scores in these assignments and exams. In hindsight, I think I worked harder at Walker's to excel academically than what I was required to at UCAB. I inferred that if Venezuela had had more excellent schools like Walker's, it would likely be a more economically developed and democratic country.

This insight sparked my interest in education. I first became interested in working to improve the school system in my home country. I had been very privileged to spend so much time in the United States and to attend an elite boarding school. And, although I wouldn't have articulated it in exactly this way, I felt compelled to devote my professional life to improving the equality of educational opportunities for children in Venezuela and the rest of the so-called developing world. I had found my passion.

When I told my father that I was going to graduate school at Duke University in Durham, North Carolina, and had secured funding from the Venezuelan government to pay my tuition and living expenses in the United States, his response was, "Why do you want to get more schooling? You're already a professional!" But after having completed a five-year college degree in communications with a minor in journalism, I did not consider myself a professional. I knew how to think and write, and I had superficial knowledge of several topics, but I did not have the in-depth knowledge or strong analytical skills that I desired. If I wanted to be well equipped to positively influence education policy, I would need more education.

My two years at Duke University were transformational. From some of the top economists in the United States, I learned how to apply economic principles to improve education policy, analyze data using statistical methods and software programs, and write memos for policymakers working within government. It was not an easy transition, as I was quickly reminded of the higher expectations top US graduate schools have as compared to top-ranking institutions in Venezuela. While my competencies in spoken and written English placed me in good stead, I lacked background knowledge of policy systems within the United States. My first memo assignment had been on the Milwaukee sewer system, and I began by looking up the word "sewer" and the location of Milwaukee. Unsurprisingly, my grades on that memo and many other earlier assignments were not in the As—as I had become so accustomed to during my undergraduate years.

During my first few months at Duke, I felt stressed and out of place. I decided to meet with the then–academic dean, Helen (Sunny) Ladd, who is a well-respected education economist. I told Sunny that the admissions committee had made a mistake in letting me in, and that this was the first time the likelihood of failing was a real possibility. She kindly reassured me that I could succeed at Duke and that I just needed to continue to diligently complete the work and be patient with my grades. If you have ever doubted that you belong, remember that you're there for a reason. And, importantly, do not be afraid to seek advice and support if you, like me, also feel overwhelmed. I now tell my new master's students, many of whom are international and feel inadequate studying at Harvard, that the admissions team knows what they are doing. They (and you) belong.

In May of 2023, my first cohort of master's students graduated from the Harvard Graduate School of Education (HGSE). One of them, a mid-career professional from India, told me that when I had reassured her that she belonged and that the admissions committee knew what it was doing, she could thereafter truly enjoy her time at Harvard—and her grades also improved.

Like this student, my grades also improved as I got the gist of it at Duke, and I began to enjoy exploring all the school had to offer. Besides completing my coursework for the master's in public policy (MPP) program, I audited development economics in the Economics Department and took advanced French classes in the Language Department. During the summer, I interned at the Research Triangle Institute's (RTI) Center for International Development, where I was exposed to the world of international development for the very first time. This internship led to a part-time job during my second year and eventually to a full-time position after I graduated in June 1993.

Once again, just as when I graduated from college, I felt that I did not have the in-depth economics and econometrics skills that I needed to independently lead the kind of research that could effectively inform education policy. I therefore decided to pursue a doctoral degree focused on the economics of education. After sending out applications to a handful of selective programs in the United States, I was thrilled to receive acceptance to the doctoral program in Administration, Planning and Social Policy at HGSE.

As soon as I arrived in Cambridge in August 1995, I felt I belonged. I loved the diversity of the students, who came from all over the United States and indeed the entire globe. I adored my apartment—a light-filled and spacious one-bedroom on the first floor of a two-family home (the owners lived in the two floors above) on Huron Avenue, right across the street from a grocery store, a small casual restaurant, and a few shops—an area known as "Huron Village."

Charlie Clotfelter, a former Duke professor and renowned education economist with whom I had remained in touch during my time working at RTI, offered me one piece of advice. He said, "If you end up going to HGSE, make sure to ask Richard [Dick] Murnane to serve as your adviser. He's not only one of the most talented economists working in education, but he's also a very kind person. I know you're shy, and you may not want to do this; but believe me, professors also like to work with nice students. You'll be doing him a favor too."

Murnane did not become my assigned adviser; however, Charlie's advice was the wind I needed at my back to later request a change in adviser. And since I barely knew the adviser that had been assigned to me, no one's feelings were hurt—at the time I was very sensitive to how others may think or feel about what I said or did. Although I still care, I have developed thicker skin over the years.

Dick Murnane was in his fifties at the time and a brilliant labor economist—indisputably one of the founders of the field of economics of education. Perhaps most notably, Dick is as kind and humble as he is accomplished—a rare combination among Ivy League professors. His corner office on the fourth floor of the Gutman Library was full of books and piles of papers—they covered the top of his desk and even the floor! I wondered how he was able to ever find anything in the chaos. He was rather miraculously always able to find the book or document that he needed—always apologizing for his messy office during the search.

At our first advising meeting, and almost every meeting thereafter, Dick asked me, "Where do you see yourself after graduation and ten years down the road? If I know what your career goals are, I'll be better positioned to advise you. But please know that you can also change your mind, and I will support you no matter what." In that first meeting and throughout my years at HGSE, I answered, "I want to be an economist of education and a professor at a great university, just like you." Getting a doctoral degree was a big investment in both time and financial resources, and I wanted to gain the skills I needed to research important policy questions independently, even if it meant (as I soon learned) starting with the very basics. For example, I took math courses at Harvard College in order to be eligible for enrollment into the graduate-level economics courses I was interested in. After my Harvard graduation, I didn't want to feel the same way I had felt after college and my MPP.

If I'm totally honest, another strong motivator for me wanting to be a professor was that, during my time at RTI, I had met a few women working in international development organizations who were also married with children. I thought that working at a university would allow me to juggle motherhood and a career more easily due to the more flexible schedule and the summer holidays, and that this may not be the case working in international development organizations. I wanted to find a partner to start a family with. I couldn't imagine not being a mother or having a family. Thus, when I first went to HGSE for my doctoral degree, my dream was to work at a US-based university during the school year and then travel to Caracas, Venezuela, during the summer breaks, possibly even leaving my future children there with my mom—who absolutely loved children! Then I could spend time traveling in Latin America to collect data for my academic research.

But, as the saying goes, "If you want God to laugh, tell him your plans."

In October 1997, as I was walking across Harvard Yard on a beautiful fall morning with the crisp air and blue skies typical that time of year, I thought of how lucky I was to be in this amazing place, learning from brilliant professors and students. I felt a deep gratitude. After having worked full-time at RTI for two years, I knew what a privilege it was to spend this amount of time learning and doing research among the best and brightest, and I wanted to make the most of my time here. I was truly happy.

That evening, I got a phone call from Caracas. It was Mom and Dad on the line, and they had also looped in my sister from New York City. They let us know that Mom had been diagnosed with lung cancer and that she would be undergoing surgery the next day to remove a tumor from one of her lungs. My sister and I begged our mom to delay the surgery by one day, to give us time to get there. The next day, we took a flight to Caracas.

At fifty-one, my mom was still a beautiful woman, slim (she exercised every weekday and avoided carbohydrates religiously) with large green eyes, a small pointed nose, and light brown wavy hair. My dad adored her. He boasted about her beauty, often telling the story of how once, at a restaurant in Paris, a man had come to their table for an autograph, thinking my mom was Catherine Deneuve. And she was equally beautiful inside. She was loving, empathetic, curious about everyone, and a great listener.

After the initial shock I'm sure she felt when told she had a tumor, she quickly sprang into action. Three of her five sisters were breast cancer survivors, and she was very optimistic that she too would survive the disease. She insisted on getting the tumor out as soon as possible, hoping it had not yet spread. And so, a day after my sister and I arrived in Caracas, we all went to the hospital to have her tumor surgically removed.

The surgery took longer than expected, as the tumor was larger than it had appeared in the X-rays. In fact, the doctors told us that they had to remove an entire lung to ensure that all the cancerous cells were taken out. They were optimistic that they had succeeded in removing all the cancerous cells, but she would need to have tests every six months to ensure she remained cancer-free.

My sister and I were skeptical of the health care in Venezuela (even of the best private doctors who were looking after Mom), and we insisted (primarily to Dad, who ultimately was the decision-maker in the family) that Mom get a second opinion. After many discussions, we convinced our parents that getting a second opinion in the United States was a wise move. They chose a doctor at the Memorial Sloan Kettering Cancer Center (MSKCC) in New York City.

Suddenly, the luxury of being able to focus exclusively on graduate school had ended. From then on, I divided my time between Cambridge, Caracas, and New York (and later Washington, DC), taking shifts with my sister to accompany Mom through numerous tests and treatments. Almost every checkup revealed a new spread of cancer. It was disheartening to see Mom go from being the happy, optimistic person she had always been to gradually shutting down, weakened by the disease, chemotherapy, and radiotherapy treatments.

Going back and forth between Caracas (where my mom got her chemotherapy), DC (where I now lived and worked), New York (where my mom went for tests and specialized treatment), and Cambridge (to meet with Dick and my other advisers, and later to teach) became the new normal. I had finished all the coursework and was working on my "qualifying paper," an analysis of the impact of a 1990s reform in Venezuela whereby the national government committed to funding Catholic schools in underserved areas. I was busy inputting data into a digital database from years of teacher payroll data in paper that the Venezuelan Association of Catholic Schools had generously shared with me for the research. I spent the bulk of the 1998–1999 school year working on this analysis and submitted (and got approved with distinction) the qualifying paper requirement in the spring semester of 1999. I was officially now a doctoral candidate (as opposed to a doctoral "student").

In the summer of 1999, I was invited to present my recently completed qualifying paper at a conference cohosted by the World Bank and the Inter-American Development Bank (IDB) in Brasilia. There, I learned that the IDB was funding a large study of teachers across several Latin American countries. Teams of local researchers were surveying large numbers of public and private school teachers in Argentina, Chile, Guatemala, Peru, the Dominican Republic, Uruguay, and Venezuela. The IDB director who was leading the study was also from Venezuela, and we had known each other for some time. I asked if he may need someone with my skills to analyze the data collected across the countries (each country team was doing it for each country) and provide a regional perspective.

What a difference it makes to be at the right place at the right time: he offered me access to the data, a small office at the IDB, and minimum pay. In exchange, I would analyze the data and produce a report on the status of public and private school teachers in Latin America. I could see the "end of the tunnel," so to speak, of my doctoral studies.

Meanwhile, my mom's disease was taking over her body. By now the cancer had spread from her lung to her bones and brain. At each report of another part of her body contaminated with cancer cells, she would ask the doctor, "On a scale of one to ten, what are the chances that the proposed treatment [chemo, radiotherapy, etc.] will cure me?" In 1997, the odds had been around seven. By the fall of 1999, we were in the one to two range. But her response was, "One is better than zero." And she submitted her body to every possible chemo and radiotherapy, until she was so weak and sick that we had to hire a nurse 24/7 to help her eat, bathe, and move from the hospital bed we had rented and put in her room to the bathroom and back.

By the fall of 1999, my sister, who was pregnant with her first child, and I took turns taking care of our mother, each one spending two weeks in Caracas and then back home (DC for me, NY for her) to try and keep our work (she was an attorney at a high-powered NYC law firm; I needed to continue advancing on my dissertation research) and relationships going strong. I was in Caracas for Thanksgiving and the first week of December; my sister arrived around December 5 and I returned to DC. My goal was to finish preparing the database of teacher information to begin analyzing it in early 1998, after spending the holidays at home. My sister had to go back on December 15 for her last medical checkup, and we would all be together for Christmas.

On Thursday, December 16, 1999, torrential rains poured over the northern coast of Venezuela, causing severe mudslides in La Guaira, the area where the Simón Bolívar International Airport is located. I called my mom on Friday, December 17, at around 10:00 a.m., just to check in and hear how she was feeling. She explained how worried she was for the thousands of poor people living in slums in La Guaira, who were losing their homes and livelihoods. Even on her deathbed, she always cared more about others than about herself.

I had planned to travel back to Caracas on Sunday, December 19, and I began to worry about flight cancellations. Venezuela was a closed economy, and many products that were widely available in the United States were impossible to buy. When I returned to DC on December 5, I had brought with me a list from several aunts and friends of things to bring back (they would all reimburse me). Initially, I was hoping to go on Saturday to buy all these things, but with the rains and all, I decided to go on Friday afternoon and to try and move up my flight to Saturday. Although I had a mobile phone, it was large and clunky (the big old Nokia phones, before the flip kind), and I only used it for emergencies. I forgot to take it with me on the errands run that afternoon.

When I got home at around 5:00 p.m., I saw the flashing red light on our voicemail machine. There were multiple missed calls from my parents' home number in Caracas and several voicemail messages. It was my dad's voice, and as I listened to message after message, I heard him asking me to call back as soon as possible. Finally, I heard the last message, "Emi, the worst has happened. Your mom died."

My mother's death had a huge impact on me. I loved her profoundly and without reservations. I had always felt her deep love for me, and her constant presence at home had been a source of comfort and confidence. She was a beautiful (inside and out) woman, a giving and gentle soul who brought joy to everyone whose life she touched. At the same time, I could tell how angry she had been toward the end that her life was being cut short, and this was very painful. Her passing taught me how fleeting life can be and the importance of being present, seizing on the joyful moments and accepting that the painful ones one day will pass. This lesson has greatly influenced my personal and professional choices.

It was certainly not my original plan to spend the bulk of my career in international development organizations. Yet, I soon discovered these were the best places for a young professional like me to be able to have a tangible impact on education policy at a large scale. Thirteen years of tertiary education (five years getting a college education, then two master's degrees [three years] and a doctorate [five]), in part, made it possible for me to secure a place in this competitive sector.

What I learned during those thirteen years of study is how crucial a high-quality education is when it comes to applying for opportunities to work within international development organizations. My continued quest after college to obtain my master's degree at Duke and even stronger skills undoubtedly played a significant role in my acceptance into the highly selective Young Professionals Program at the World Bank immediately after I graduated from Harvard.

A high-quality education, however, is a great deal more than mere coursework. Even as a student, building networks of like-minded professionals is crucial. Without necessarily having a specific agenda, I regularly reached out to former professors and colleagues to fill them in on my whereabouts and, more importantly, ask them about their movements and present work. These efforts led to connection after connection and opened many doors for me. Most importantly, it resulted in a large network of mentors from whom I could seek guidance—including the likes of Dick Murnane. Many of these mentors later become professional collaborators and personal friends.

To truly make the most of one's connections, especially in international development, it's important to demonstrate both your passion for the cause *and* your skills. Young people, typically undergraduate or master's students with only a few years of work experience, have often asked me for advice on how to secure a job in an IDO. They highlight their passion for international development, poverty reduction, improving educational opportunities, and the like. I understand and relate to their genuine, passionate personal convictions about needing to improve international education, and indeed I wish to help them make this a reality. However, passion alone is not sufficient. Acquiring the hard and soft skills that are needed to work within international development organizations cannot be overstated. I worked long and hard hours to get to where I needed to be, driven by the desire to help bring about positive tangible change in developing country education.

The good news is that determination and hard work pay off!

If you're a college student considering starting a career in international development, how should you spend your time in college? My advice is to take as many social science courses as you are able, for example, economics, public policy analysis, and sociology. Combine these subject areas with the hard(er) skills of math, statistics, data analysis, and econometrics so that you may qualify for entry-level research assistant positions or consulting jobs within IDOs. And, it may seem obvious, but work on becoming fluent in a second (or third) language. To work in international development, I have found some of the most useful languages to know are Arabic, French, and Spanish.

One area I did not pursue while in graduate school is the field of development economics. At Harvard and in many other great universities, there are social scientists whose work solely focuses on understanding issues of poverty and economic development in low- and middle-income countries (LMICs). I did not take any courses in development economics, in part because I decided to focus on the core courses of microeconomics, labor economics, and econometrics, which my advisers had also recommended. Furthermore, I thought that I knew "development" because I had been born and raised in a developing country and had some work experience in development while at RTI. In hindsight, I missed out on learning more about development issues, and perhaps even more important, connecting with influential thought-leaders in this field earlier on in my career. Fortunately, at the World Bank I was able to meet and work alongside many of them. My recommendation to students is that they enroll in development economics courses as soon as possible, especially if they have not already spent a significant amount of time living in a low- or middle-income country.

I also urge students to take advantage of the summer breaks by exploring living and working in LMICs. There are many organizations to choose from, including those mentioned in chapter 1, "The Basics of IDOs," that offer field-based internships for college students. The combination of academic knowledge and skill in relevant disciplines together with firsthand experience working within LMICs makes for a very attractive candidate for early career opportunities.

I would be remiss if I did not urge young people, if truly serious about a career in institutions like the WB and other multilateral or bilateral international organizations, to start thinking about graduate school options sooner rather than later.

If you are a master's or doctoral student looking to embark on a career in an international development organization, I advise you not to take shortcuts. Don't merely enroll in courses that are more likely to yield you higher grades—take courses that are challenging and offer you the most learning. Take full advantage of being in graduate school to master the social science and data analysis skills that you'll need. Connect with professors, faculty members, mentors, and students who are working or have already worked in the field of international education and begin investing in a professional network that you can later tap into during the course of your career. I can't emphasize this latter point enough.

Are you a mid-career professional looking to make a career shift to international development organizations? Ideally, you have some of the technical and language skills that I have mentioned above. If this is not the case, however, there are many online courses that you can take to acquire (or refresh) them. You may need to make a lateral move, or even be prepared to accept a lower position to begin with; however, if you're both passionate *and* competent, you're likely to swiftly advance and thrive within the sector.

3

Standing Out from the Crowd

This is a great start, really excellent! I just have a few suggestions.

—Luis Crouch

The first time that Luis Crouch, my supervisor at Research Triangle Institute's Center for International Development, where I had my first internship, gave me feedback on my writing, he first gave me a figurative pat on the back. Then, he proceeded to walk me through each line. Little by little, he explained ways in which I needed to include evidence or to write more compellingly.

I clearly understood that my draft had not been up to expectations; however, I didn't feel terrible. Luis understood that I was a fresh master's graduate with potential. He gave me an opportunity and actively supported my professional growth along the way. I knew that when "I grew up," I wanted to be just like him: mentoring young people with both kindness and rigor. From then on, I have strived to maintain this approach.

During my time at RTI, I traveled to many countries and regions of the world, including Africa (Ethiopia and Tanzania), the Middle East (Egypt and Tunisia), and South America (Ecuador). Most of the projects in which I worked were funded by USAID and the World Bank, and I became increasingly fascinated by the world of international development.

I was not working exclusively on education-related challenges. As I explained in chapter 1, "The Basics of IDOs," most IDOs within the *advisers* category work across a wide range of different sectors and regions of the world. Many of RTI's projects addressed issues such as family planning, urban planning, health, and education. My role was to support the more senior staff by reviewing the literature, analyzing data, and preparing draft presentations and reports whose intended audiences were often government decision-makers.

In 1994, I worked on a project in Ecuador, which required an analysis of the quality and equity of primary education with a specific focus on the roles of private and public schools. It was a USAID-funded project, and RTI was a subcontractor to another firm based in Washington, DC. Luis led the analytical process, including identifying the research questions, research methods, and key findings. I would follow his instructions and use my recently acquired statistical skills to analyze the data. I could interpret the output of the statistical programs we were using to summarize the key findings into draft reports and prepare draft presentations (back then, we used a software called Harvard Graphics, a precursor to today's MS PowerPoint). However, I could see that, unlike Luis, I was not yet able to independently devise research questions and identify the best methods to analyze data.

I wanted to learn these skills, and that is one of the reasons why I went to Harvard.

While I was studying at Harvard, another graduate student connected me to an economist working in the education unit of the Latin America region at the World Bank. He was looking for research assistance to contribute to a study on teacher pay conditions in Argentina and asked me to go to the Bank's website and apply to the WB's Summer Internships Program. Later, I learned that many students from all over the world apply for a limited number of summer intern positions and that team leaders across the WB have specific needs and may find it difficult to find a suitable candidate. Having had this connection proved crucial, as I was offered one of the highly competitive WB summer internships to work on the project. This opportunity allowed me to get my feet wet in work that was closely aligned with my research goals and interests.

The WB's headquarters are spread across several buildings in the heart of DC. My office was in the Main Complex (MC)—a large, modern building occupying an entire block between H and G Streets just two blocks from the White House. The MC used to be composed of four separate buildings that were later redesigned and connected, creating a large, bright interior atrium with a glass ceiling. It is truly stunning, and after passing through security each day, I felt inspired by the big sign on the wall that read "Our Dream Is a World Free of Poverty."

My direct supervisor, Lant Pritchett, was a young economist known at the WB and among other development economists for thinking "outside the box." A medium-sized man, likely in his late thirties at the time, bald and with a little hair left that he tied back into a ponytail, Lant dressed casually (by WB standards back then) and enjoyed instigating controversial discussions. More importantly, he deeply cared about development and, especially, education and considered it a crucial means to promote prosperity—for both individuals and societies at large. Right from the beginning, he and I got along well, and he has remained a colleague, mentor, and friend ever since.

In July 1997, we traveled to Argentina as part of a supervision mission of a WB loan to the province of Buenos Aires. This was my first trip to Buenos Aires, and I was taken aback by its old and beautiful European-style buildings and climate—that there are four distinct seasons (unlike the two—rainy or dry—seasons in Venezuela). I was also awed by the very different trees and flowers, some of which I had never seen before. Everything about Argentina was distinct from Venezuela and Ecuador, the only two South American countries I had been to. Furthermore, the Spanish that Argentinians speak differs significantly from the Venezuelan Spanish I was accustomed to. For example, the way that verbs are conjugated, and the way *ll* is pronounced as *ch* instead of the softer *y* in Venezuela; even some vocabulary is completely different.

One day, as the WB team members and our counterparts from the government of Argentina were walking together down a busy city street, I saw a food cart with a sign that read "*Vendo maní.*" I asked my Argentinian colleague, "What is *maní* here?" Using his fingers, he tried to show what a peanut looks like, and settled on the Spanish-Castillian term *cacahuete*. I replied, "Ah, it's the same as in Venezuela!" Exasperated, he turned to me and asked, "Then, why did you ask?" I replied, "I am so confused by now by the linguistic differences that I didn't want to make any assumptions." Despite numerous superficial differences, I immediately felt comfortable due to our similar histories and the Spanish language, which allowed me to foster strong personal and professional relationships with Argentinians.

The capital of the province of Buenos Aires, La Plata, is located about an hour's drive from the city of Buenos Aires, through monotonous flat fields. Unlike Buenos Aires, which is full of majestic buildings and beautiful lively streets lined with restaurants, shops, and cafes, La Plata was dull in comparison. The province's Ministry of Education was, and I think still is, located within a classic 1970s-style building—a block of concrete bricks. In the middle of the lobby, there was a small office with a wooden window with jail-like bars, wherein a thin man, probably in his forties, sat working behind a desk full of dozens of stacks of letter-sized paper. Those papers were the pay stubs for the entire province's teacher workforce, and one man was single-handedly responsible for keeping account of them all.

It was not surprising after observing this lone worker in a room full of paper that the World Bank had discovered a significant numbers of "ghost" teachers in Argentina. These were teachers who were included on the province's payroll and thus received salaries, but never actually showed up to work, an issue that is all too common across developing countries. Addressing the problem of "ghost" teachers was one of the reasons the WB was attempting to finance the establishment of a centralized, digital teacher payroll management system. Here I learned an important lesson: creating an automated and electronic system to manage teacher pay was not merely a technical challenge, but also a deeply political challenge. Many corrupt individuals, including teachers, administrators, and politicians, were benefiting from the existing manual system and were thus resistant to change. Many years later, in March 2016, I returned to the Ministry of Education in La Plata as Division Chief of Education at the Inter-American Development Bank (IDB). The same bizarre room, filled with stacks of pay stubs, was still there; the challenge had managed to endure.

The following day, back in the city of Buenos Aires, we visited the National Ministry of Education to meet with Alejandro (Ale), a young Argentinian economist responsible for managing all the Ministry of Education's data. I remember spending hours with him in the Palacio Pizzurno—a very old and beautiful European-style palace in the heart of the city, within which the ministry's headquarters was located. In his small, windowless, and cigarette-smoke-filled office, I explained to him that we were interested in researching the extent to which teachers were being over- or underpaid in Argentina. This topic was relevant at the time, as the country's central government was in the midst of difficult negotiations with the national teachers' union regarding teacher pay and working conditions. Once Ale understood that we might be able to help the government of Argentina by providing evidence that teachers may not actually be paid less than workers in similar occupations, he managed to provide us with the necessary data. (Many years later, I would be Ale's boss at the IDB.)

With valuable data in hand, we returned to Washington, DC, and worked long hours analyzing it. We produced a research paper that found that the number of hours that teachers were expected to work (considering the nine-month school year, public holidays, and school vacations) meant that their hourly pay was at least as good as, if not better than, that of employees with similar demographics, educational attainments, and work experience. Our paper was used as a reference during the negotiations between the government of Argentina and the national teachers' union.

I was thrilled that my emerging research skills had been useful to inform important policy decisions. During this summer internship, I became even more convinced that further developing data analysis and research skills would enable me to be even more impactful in positively shaping global education policies. My efforts to focus on strengthening these skills at Harvard were crucial in helping me enter the highly competitive Young Professionals Program at the WB.

How did I get into the renowned YPP, for which many other applicants had similar academic backgrounds and experiences? As is almost always the case, I think it was a combination of the quality of my résumé and some, or perhaps a great deal of, luck.

My early professional experiences shaped both me and my goals. I found and spent time learning from mentors, witnessed policymaking in action, and began to understand the nature of the challenges and possibilities that lay ahead of me on this career path. Most importantly, *I learned that while acquiring sophisticated technical skills was necessary to do the work, it was not sufficient. To be effective, one also needs to have the communication, interpersonal, and political skills to navigate complex systems.*

Indeed, in my first mission with the WB, I quickly realized that there is something invaluably special about being fully fluent and being able to use culturally appropriate humor to successfully forge the kinds of interpersonal connections necessary for effective professional and personal relationships within international development projects.

Many years after I had worked with Lant Pritchett as a summer intern at the World Bank, he told me that in the recommendation letter he had written for me when I applied to the YPP, he described a specific instance during our mission to Argentina. We were on our way to a meeting with government officials, and I asked if we could stop to buy delicious mini-croissants and sugar cookies, coated with chocolate and dulce de leche—known as *facturas* in Argentina. I explained that in every other meeting we had attended that week, our counterparts had brought pastries for us, and I thought it would be good for us to return the favor. In Lant's letter, as he now shared with me, he had noted that from that day during my summer internship, he knew I should be accepted into the WB's YPP. While many other YPP applicants had similar technical and language skills, my interpersonal skills had set me apart.

To be sure, throughout my career, I have met too many early career professionals who could successfully be engaged with their supervisors and yet failed to work productively alongside their peers. In the worst of cases, they were outright rude and disrespectful to their subordinates within the corporate hierarchy. Time and time again I observed that, regardless of how intelligent or talented they were, they had limited careers within IDOs and, as a result, impact.

Many young professionals aspire to work in IDOs, yet there are few staff vacancies each year. Understanding how to stand out from the crowd when applying will increase your chances of success.

How to Progress within IDOs

I am often asked by college or master's students how I progressed to where I am in my career. In response, I emphasize three necessary skills: deep *technical skills* (for me this took the form of economics training applied to education; however, for you it may be another field entirely); the *ability to work effectively with diverse people* (individuals from diverse cultures and contexts, with varied working styles and skill sets); and the *capacity to deliver quality products that comply with the allocated budgets and timelines.* These three skills are crucial for working for the different types of IDOs described here.

The vast majority of staff and consultants working in the technical track (in research and operations) in multilateral development banks are trained in economics. The bottom line is that these are indeed financial institutions, where an understanding of economics and finance is a prerequisite for most positions.

Even if you do not become an economist, you will need to speak and understand the language of economists to succeed in the world of international development. You'll need to have a basic understanding of how financial markets work and how to analyze the (opportunity) costs and benefits as well as the potential trade-offs of alternative programs and policies. I was fortunate to learn this early on in my career when, while at RTI, I realized that although I wanted to conduct research that would inform education policymakers, I still lacked the conceptual frameworks and analytical skills to do so effectively. I spent most of my time at Harvard developing my economics and econometrics (statistics) skills; however, my colleagues who joined the World Bank, having studied at other graduate schools of education, had had some previous study or work experience in economics or public policy.

The "T" Profile

For the most competitive entry-level positions, like the Young Professionals Program, recruiters sought out what they referred to as a "T" profile. The vertical line of the *T* represents depth in a specific field or sector, for example, a deep knowledge about the areas of health, education, or finance. Possessing an advanced graduate degree, such as a PhD, signals the depth of your expertise.

I am often invited to speak to master's students graduating from top universities in the USA, including my alma mater, Duke's Sanford Institute of Public Policy. Now, in my role as a professor at HGSE, many of my students enrolled in our program are interested in pivoting toward a career in international development.

My advice to master's students? If you're serious about pursuing a career in IDOs, get your doctoral degree as soon as possible. You may be able to begin as a short-term consultant with a master's degree, and slowly progress to an open-ended, international staff position—the operative word being "slowly." A PhD will open more doors sooner, and because it does take time to complete a doctoral degree, the sooner you begin yours, the sooner you are likely to reap the benefits in terms of better career prospects.

The shorter horizontal line across the *T* represents one's ability to make connections across different sectors. For example, you may be working on a project to improve the developmental outcomes of young children before they enter school. This kind of project may include issues related to health and nutrition, parental training, and even the expansion of access to quality childcare. Thinking too narrowly as an education specialist may cause you to focus only on expanding access to quality childcare centers, while overlooking the crucial significance of healthcare and nutrition, and the quality of parental care, for healthy early childhood development.

My advice to pursue a PhD as soon as possible practically guarantees an employer that you have a certain depth of knowledge within a specific field—health, public policy, education, etc. And, while pursuing a PhD, you could (as I did) gain relevant work experience as an intern or external consultant for faculty or IDOs whose projects are interesting and interdisciplinary. In short, take advantage of your time in graduate school to acquire both a deep specialized knowledge and a thorough understanding of the complexity and connections across multiple sectors.

If a PhD is out of the question for you, there are other ways to get your foot in the door of an IDO. Experience in government—for example, working as an adviser to a cabinet secretary or leading an evaluation unit—is highly valued by IDOs. Since the work of IDOs involves working closely with governments across the globe, prior knowledge about how governments *really* work is at least as valuable as, if not more valuable than, a PhD. Even so, today's reality is that more and more individuals have both PhDs *and* government work experience—making for a highly competitive job market.

While a strong "T" profile will likely get you in the door, to truly have an impact once you're inside requires you to be a strong communicator of data and technical concepts. My final piece of advice on how to stand out from the crowd is to *become a strong writer and translator of evidence into promising and viable policy recommendations*. IDOs are large bureaucracies that demand a lot of documentation; your tasks will likely include preparing project concept notes, project appraisal documents, project completion reports, etc. While you will never work on these tasks alone, since all work at IDOs is completed by teams of at least three technical- and support-staff members as well as several consultants, the more clearly, concisely, and compellingly you can communicate in writing, the more likely you will succeed in achieving your desired impact.

I have emphasized the importance of developing skills in the social sciences, in data analysis, and in foreign languages. These are critical ingredients for being considered for technical jobs within IDOs; however, they are certainly not sufficient. What may set you apart from competing candidates with similar skills is your ability to relate well with others, to communicate effectively—both orally and in writing, and in multiple languages—to respect and understand different cultures, and to demonstrate an ability to establish and maintain effective working relationships with people from all around the globe.

4

The Paths Worth Taking

On September 10, 2001, my first day as part of the Young Professionals Program (YPP), I arrived at the World Bank's Main Complex (MC) at around 8:30 a.m. and was welcomed by a human resources officer who accompanied me to the training room for orientation. There, I met the other thirty-one Young Professionals (YPs), who had come from all over the world. While most of us were economists, there was also an anthropologist, a sociologist, and a few lawyers.

Our first day was filled with presentations by senior managers who each shared perspectives on different aspects of the organization. We were treated to lunch in the formal dining room, where the most senior staff often share meals with distinguished guests such as government ministers and heads of state. The WB's president, Jim Wolfensohn, also made an appearance that afternoon to welcome us. We were treated like VIPs.

I was excited to begin my career, but I also felt torn about having to leave my almost six-month-old baby, Tobias, at home with a caregiver—whom we were sharing with another family. During the previous six months, I had been completely devoted to caring for him, nursing him, learning his cues—and loving every minute of being his mom. His big turquoise blue eyes and his constant smile had won me over immediately. He was also a very easygoing baby. The only challenge we experienced was that he would only fall asleep when I held him in my arms, rocking him back and forth to music for at least half an hour. Although I absolutely loved holding him in my arms, I quickly realized that nursing and cuddling and singing him to sleep at least twice during the night, and then having to go to work the next day, was absolutely exhausting!

After nine months of having to wake up multiple times during the night to soothe Tobias, we decided to implement the "Solve Your Child's Sleep Problems" method by Dr. Richard Ferber. The method involves going to the child when he cries in the middle of the night, gently and lovingly reassuring him that he is fine, and then walking away without taking him out of the crib or feeding him. Parents are supposed to increase the time that they let the child cry, to "train" the child to go back to sleep on their own. As you can imagine, Tobias—like most babies who before then had been quickly picked up out of the crib and fed back to sleep—was very upset when we walked out of the room, and he cried and cried. It was so emotionally difficult for me to hear him cry and not be able to hold and soothe him that, after the first night, I went downstairs to the office and shut the door so that I would not hear his cries. But, by the third night, it worked, and Tobias slept peacefully throughout the night ever since. I don't recommend this approach to new parents. In fact, with my second son, Emilio, I discovered that most babies could fall asleep on their own—they don't *need* the singing and rocking!

During our second day of orientation, September 11, 2001, a historic terrorist attack took place in the United States. At around 10:00 a.m., our YP orientation leader informed us of the news, and we were instructed to leave the building and the area of downtown Washington, DC, as soon as possible. At the time, one of the hijacked planes, which later crashed in southwestern Pennsylvania, was still in the air and headed toward DC. I walked to the parking garage where I had left my car, right between the Bank's MC and the White House. A long queue of people, also waiting to retrieve their cars from the public garage, stood before me. As I waited in line, a White House guard came and strongly advised us all to leave immediately—that we were risking our lives for our cars. In shock, I started walking up 19th Street toward my home, which was five miles away. I don't remember exactly how I was able to hail a taxi, but I remember the driver picking me up and telling me he was headed in the direction of my home. On our way, we picked up a few more women walking in the same direction.

With everyone in a rush to leave downtown DC, the traffic was heavy. It took us over an hour to reach my home—a trip that usually took me twenty to thirty minutes. Throughout the ride, all I could think of was how excited I was to be able to return home and hold Tobias. I don't think I was feeling fear, as the whole thing was so surreal, and the news reports were only beginning to piece together the events and make sense. Rather, I was very anxious to return home because I had missed being with my baby so much throughout the full days of orientation. I was also worried about how the new caregiver was taking care of him.

Tobias's caregiver resigned as soon as I arrived home that day. She explained that looking after two babies was too much and, in some ways, I was grateful to be free to seek out a caregiver who would focus exclusively on my child. Fortunately, the WB remained closed for some time after the tragic 9/11 attacks, which meant I could stay home to be with Tobias and sort out his care arrangements.

Over the next few days, as the WB remained closed, I stayed home watching the news and waiting for our lives to resume. On one of those days, I took Tobias to the local park and met some other parents and caregivers. At the park, and thanks to the guidance of other parents and caregivers, I found a loving caregiver for Tobias—a Chilean college graduate who was taking a career break for personal reasons and was willing to take a short-term position as a daytime caregiver. She was exactly what I had been looking for; she knew how to play and stimulate young children, she kept a detailed journal of everything Tobias did while I was at work, and she was well connected to other caregivers in the neighborhood. It was with great relief that I could now feel comfortable leaving Tobias at home during the day while I began my career at the World Bank.

The Young Professionals Program(s)

The Young Professionals Program is the best way to enter and develop professionally within the World Bank. The United Nations and several regional development banks have programs similar to the WB's YPP. These programs are often the most selective and competitive pathways into these IDOs.

Each year, over ten thousand young professionals under thirty-two years of age apply for between thirty and forty openings at the World Bank. Since the YPP is so selective, the Bank (and other IDOs with these types of programs) invests heavily in training and other professional development opportunities for its Young Professionals to ensure they stay in the organization and thrive. Many of them continue to establish successful careers in the World Bank Group (which includes not just the WB, but also the International Finance Corporation and other institutions, as explained in chapter 1, "The Basics of IDOs"). When I joined in 2001, approximately 70 percent of the WB's senior management were former YPs.

These programs recruit young professionals who are citizens of all member countries and, notably, *only* of member countries. For example, if you are from Latin America, as I am, you will not qualify to work at the Asian Development Bank or the African Development Bank. And, even if you are *very* qualified, these IDOs prefer to hire cohorts that are representative of many member countries. For instance, if you're an Indian or US citizen, you're likely to compete in a larger pool of similarly qualified young professionals for a mere one or two openings.

Each year, the incoming cohort of YPs at the WB takes part in a joint two-week-long orientation program to introduce the recruits to the basic workings of the Bank. Thereafter, each YP begins their yearlong first rotation, followed by a second yearlong rotation; finally, the YP graduates begin a "permanent" assignment, which may be in one of the two units where the rotations took place or in a new unit. The quotation marks speak to the opportunity that YPs must progress within the World Bank, while in keeping with rotation requirements for all international staff that I explained in chapter 3, "Standing Out from the Crowd."

I was thrilled that my first rotation assignment was in the WB's Development Economics Research Group (DECRG), under the supervision of a well-known economist, Beth King. I was looking forward to conducting research and publishing in academic journals. In the long term, I aspired to leverage this experience as a stepping stone toward working in academia, based at a university in the DC area. Beth was an expert at applying for internal funds to conduct large-scale research projects. Together we submitted a funding proposal to study teacher incentive reforms that had recently taken place in several countries around the world. This kind of research excited me, as it offered the opportunity to write articles for leading academic journals. It was the kind of research I would have loved to conduct for my doctoral dissertation—if I had had access to this kind of data and funding. My job was now enabling me to conduct this kind of cutting-edge research—I was thrilled!

However, I soon discovered that the daily life of a researcher was relatively lonely and isolating. I hated leaving Tobias at home with a caregiver, as great as she was, to spend most of the day analyzing data and attempting to write research papers alone in my windowless office. To compound these feelings there were no concrete deadlines or clients who were interested in making use of my research findings. Unlike many of my colleagues who were introverts and preferred working alone, I'm an extrovert and thrive when interacting with people.

For the first time in my, albeit short, professional life, I began to dislike going to work. I recalled my dad's feedback early on in my career and the lesson I had drawn—a job should be enjoyable at least 70 percent of the time, and the other 30 percent is why we get paid. *Even as an early career professional, once the share of interesting work in a particular job drops to less than 70 percent, it is time to move on.*

The second YP rotation couldn't come soon enough. I was assigned to the education sector within the Human Development (HD) Department of the Middle East and North Africa (MENA) region. My supervisor, the education sector manager, asked me to contribute to the education sector review of Morocco. The work also involved the design of a new loan from the WB to help expand and improve basic quality education in Tunisia. During this rotation, I also had the opportunity to travel to Morocco as part of a WB mission.

While on this assignment, I found my groove at the World Bank. I truly enjoyed conducting research and analysis when it was to inform policy within a specific country. I loved interacting with the policymakers from the client countries. Hearing directly from them about the unique challenges their countries were facing, and tapping into the WB's ample resources, was exciting. As a multilateral IDO, we had access to immense amounts of data as well as policy-relevant research from all over the globe. And, so, we were able to present them with the best global evidence to inform their decisions.

My second rotation was to conclude just short of a year, as I was expecting my second child and would soon go on maternity leave. Emilio was born on January 20, 2003, a healthy boy with big brown eyes and dark hair. While I had been quietly worried about the prospect of loving another child as much as I loved Tobias, my apprehension was swept away as soon as Emilio was born. He instantly won me over with his smiles, easygoing nature, and ability (which became evident soon enough) to make us laugh. I felt like the size of my heart had quite literally doubled.

Knowing that my work involved frequent travel out of the country and now with two young children, we decided to seek a full-time, live-in nanny. A benefit for international staff in some IDOs, especially the WB, International Monetary Fund, and Inter-American Development Bank, is that you may sponsor a foreign person for a "domestic employee" visa to come live in the United States. Having lived so many years outside my own country, I did not know anyone from Venezuela who could fulfill this role. But, because these institutions are all based within a short radius in downtown Washington, DC, there is a market of individuals who are already in the city and who, for one or another reason (often because their sponsor is moving out of the United States), are looking for work. Luckily, through my Venezuelan friends working in these institutions, I met a Colombian national who was interested in working as a nanny for us. Dolly joined our family a few months before Emilio was born and stayed with us for thirteen years until I could no longer financially justify keeping a full-time nanny. Up to the present, she is part of our family, and both boys consider her a second mother.

Professionally, being in the YPP opened doors internally, as my work in research and project operations in the MENA region had not gone unnoticed. For my first permanent assignment after graduating from the YPP, I was offered a position as an education economist in the Human Development Department of the Latin America and Caribbean (LAC) region. I took this position for three reasons. First, I was keen on working on education issues in Latin America—my region of origin. Second, I had heard through the grapevine that the director of the HD Department in LAC was a progressive female leader, who promoted a healthy "work-life balance" and rewarded performance, as opposed to merely the number of hours spent working. As a mother of two young children, I needed this kind of flexibility and understanding—to be both the mother and professional that I hoped to be. Third, the traveling distances and time differences between Washington, DC, Latin America, and the Caribbean are the shortest among all the World Bank's regions, which made the amount of time I spent traveling and in the DC office much more manageable. (If, for example, you are based in the WB's headquarters in Washington, DC, but work with East or South Asian countries, you will need to be at the office early in the mornings and/or late in the evenings to hold calls with colleagues and counterparts, which in turn influences the time you may spend at home with family.)

Navigating Fixed-Term and Open-Ended Positions

Fortunately, besides the YPP, there are many other paths to IDOs. *Fixed-term* (usually three- or four-year-long appointments) and *open-ended* (which has no end date, and dismissal typically only happens under severe grounds) positions for sector specialists open regularly. It is best to regularly check the IDOs' websites, as new positions are always posted there. These positions are indeed also very competitive, and like the YPP, they too offer attractive professional development opportunities, compensation, and benefits. In chapter 3, "Standing Out from the Crowd," I reviewed the types of positions and skills needed to land a job in most IDOs.

Once you secure a staff (local or international) position, which may be fixed-term or open-ended, you will participate in an annual performance evaluation process. In most IDOs, this involves preparing a self-evaluation, usually through an online platform using a specific template, and selecting three to five peer reviewers from the colleagues with whom you closely worked throughout the year. This evaluation is then submitted to your direct supervisor who, along with the rest of the management team, determines your pay increases, promotions, and bonuses, as well as provides feedback during one-on-one meetings.

I was a YP in the research department (which is initially a fixed-term, two-year, renewable international staff position, after which, if you secure a "permanent assignment," it becomes an open-ended staff position) when I first participated in the performance evaluation process, and I was fortunate that my direct supervisor returned the form to me and instructed me on how better to explain—and further highlight—my contributions. She explained that these evaluations would remain as part of my professional records throughout my career within the WB and that they should not be taken lightly. I learned that a series of strong annual evaluations is key to securing a promotion.

As a conscientious and high-achieving worker, I was used to receiving positive feedback from my peers, which is why I was particularly stunned when, during my second year in the Latin America and Caribbean region, my supervisor informed me that several of my colleagues had said that I could sometimes be aloof. I had to look up the word *aloof* in the dictionary and was shocked to learn that I could come across as snobbish and standoffish. After the initial shock and upon further reflection, I realized that I could become impatient with colleagues whom I perceived as not being the most intelligent, committed, or hardworking. While I was never obviously impolite, I had not considered them as seriously as I had other colleagues for whom I had more respect.

Over time, I became more grateful to have received this kind of feedback so early on in my career. I now know that every organization has its share of high, average, and low performers; however, *the quality of a person goes beyond their work, and everyone deserves to be considered and respected.* This lesson made me a better professional, colleague, and, later, manager. From then on, even if I did not equally value everyone's work, I was more intentional about not sharing my true opinions (even if just through facial gestures) with those peers whose work or contributions I did not judge as especially valuable. Later, when I became a manager, I learned to convey my expectations and encourage everyone to do their best, and I learned how to give constructive feedback when their work did not meet my expectations. I strived to apply what I had learned from Luis Crouch in the early days of my career, to be both kind and rigorous.

SHORT- AND EXTENDED-TERM CONSULTANCIES

I want to highlight *short-term consultancies*, which are available in most IDOs and often lead to longer-term positions. These can be as short as three months; however, they may be renewed based on the quality of the work provided. These organizations have many short-term needs, such as a literature review, an economic analysis as part of the project preparation, or database construction. The largest number of openings at IDOs take the form of these consultancy contracts. Many senior specialists I worked alongside over the years would say that they had begun on a three-month contract—fifteen or twenty years before!

I hired many early career professionals as short-term consultants over the years. At one point I was so desperate to get help for a project that I hired someone on the spot, or at least after double-checking with her then-supervisor. She was the first person to walk into my office, and a consultant who had been working down the hall for another team leader (TL) and whose project and funding were coming to an end. After working with me for a couple of years, she won an open-ended position through a competitive process and went on to have a long and successful career at the World Bank.

Here's my advice—even if you're very risk-averse, consider taking on a short-term consultancy role if you are looking for ways to get your foot in the door at an IDO. If you're both hardworking and competent, it will more likely than not serve as a valuable stepping stone toward securing a long-term position.

TAKING ADVANTAGE OF PROFESSIONAL GROWTH OPPORTUNITIES

Once hired in an IDO, whether as a permanent staff member or as a consultant, you will have countless opportunities to learn and grow professionally. Every week there are typically several "brown bag lunches" during which experts give presentations on any number of development issues. Most of the time, they are free and open to all staff and consultants. Practically, you could attend a brown bag lunch every day; however, my advice is to be selective, as you should also utilize your lunch hour to build relationships with your colleagues.

There will usually be several formal events throughout the year where high-level speakers are invited to present to the entire WB community. These speakers may include former heads of state, current cabinet members, and professors from top universities across the world. While at the WB, I recall a particularly interesting presentation by Michael Porter, a Harvard Business School professor and organizational management expert, who was advising on yet another reorganization of the WB (the periodic reorganizations, or shake-ups, of IDOs is a topic for another book).

The renowned education economist Eric Hanushek, a senior fellow at Stanford University's Hoover Institution and recipient of the 2021 Yidan Prize for Education Research, also made an appearance at one of our Human Development Weeks—an annual retreat of all WB staff working in the HD Department. His presentation was about his early work on the relationship between the quality of education and economic development. I have since used his research to make the case for countries to increase their financial investments in education.

Another brown bag lunch presentation that I will never forget, for very different reasons, was by Nancy Birdsall, founder of the Center for Global Development. She had previously worked at the World Bank and had also been the executive vice president of the Inter-American Development Bank. I don't remember the details of her presentation; however, I have never forgotten that, in the very middle of her talk, her cell phone rang and she actually answered it! She spoke lovingly with her family in front of all of us and, after hanging up, just continued with her talk. I thought to myself, "Wow, I guess that's what you can do once you're that accomplished!"

I also remember hearing Nicholas Negroponte during one of the Human Development Weeks. As the founder of the MIT Media Lab, which led the development of the One Laptop per Child project, he told the World Bank's education staff that children in sub-Saharan Africa would learn more by using a laptop under a tree. Specifically, that children would learn more from laptops like the ones produced by the MIT Media Lab than by having a physical classroom and teacher.[1] While I think he should be commended for having the vision for technology companies to produce low-cost laptops and tablets, his idea that technology would replace teachers and schools has been proven wrong, as demonstrated by education lapses during the COVID-19 pandemic.

As an early career professional in an IDO, you are expected to manage your career development. This means spending time networking to find your next opportunity as either a consultant or regular staff. An unwritten rule is that you *must tell your direct supervisor*, who is often the team leader who hired you, that you are pursuing other opportunities. In the internal market within an IDO, if a TL finds out that one of their consultants is approaching other TLs for consultancy work without having been informed directly, this becomes a crime equivalent to treason! More likely than not, when working as a consultant, your TL will be asked to provide references to the following TL. So, it is in your best interest to remain transparent with your TL during your job searches.

To sum up, if you manage to land an opportunity like becoming one of the WB's or another IDO's Young Professionals, that's wonderful! However, there are plenty of other possible pathways into IDOs, from short-term consultancies to open-ended positions. If you have a sought-after set of skills and strong networks, you are likely to be able to make your way in. I chose to write this book to offer readers, especially those not familiar with the world of IDOs, an insider's perspective. I also hope to inspire passionate young people, irrespective of background, to gain the kinds of skills, experiences, and relationships that would likely lead to a rewarding and impactful career in international development.

Part II

How You Thrive

5

Navigating the Matrix

It's a bit crazy that the Bank exerts so much effort each year in recruiting a new cohort of Young Professionals and two years later, we all have to find a new job.

—Emmanuela Di Gropello

While getting into the Young Professionals Program is a great feat, finding your first assignment after the YPP, and indeed each one thereafter, requires significant and strategic effort. As I write this book, I realize this is true of all international staff in IDOs, not just the YPP alumni.

Over time my work in the development banks, specifically the World Bank and the Inter-American Development Bank, led to more experience and seniority. This allowed me to also engage closely with United Nations (UN) education-related agencies, such as the UN Education Science and Culture Organization (UNESCO), its International Institute for Education Planning (IIEP), and the UN Children's Fund (UNICEF), as well as the Brookings Institution's Center for Universal Education (CUE) and several regional banks like the Asian Development Bank (ADB). I presently serve as an expert adviser to large international consulting firms that work with governments to improve education systems, as well as on the Governing Board of the UNESCO International Institute for Education Planning, on the Global Advisory Council of the Organization of Ibero-American States (OEI), and the

Board of Directors of the Jacobs Foundation—one of the world's largest philanthropic foundations focused on global education.

Suffice it to say, I gained significant exposure to these institutions and their organizational structures. More often than not, this took the form of the "matrix."

What is the matrix? The matrix is the most common organizational structure of development banks and other IDOs. Like in a spreadsheet, in the matrix geographical departments and units are in the columns and sectoral departments and units are in the rows. In this type of organization, staff work in (are "mapped to") both technical (sectors, such as health and education) and geographical departments and thus report to two (sometimes more) supervisors. In this chapter, I share how it works and how best to navigate it—from the time of your first assignment through to how to progress toward increasing levels of responsibility and even greater impact. I will then discuss the role of the Board of Directors, which is where the technical and the political spheres of IDOs most clearly intersect.

How the Matrix Works

Because IDOs focus on numerous regions and subregions of the world, most assign staff to work in specific geographies on specific sectoral topics. Within individual countries and across regions, these institutions provide financial and technical assistance across multiple sectors, ranging from human development (or the social sectors) to infrastructure (energy, water, transportation), including both the public and the private sectors.

Based on your technical expertise, indicated by your graduate degree and previous experience, you'll work on a specific sector and geography, or the so-called Global Practice for your sector. Throughout most of my career, I intentionally worked within the education sector, which is part of a larger department at the WB called the Human Development (HD) Department. At the IDB it is called the Social Sector, which also includes health, social protection, and labor. In some institutions, this sector also includes the team working on gender, diversity, and inclusion.

At the WB, each sector and geography is grouped under vice presidencies. There are regional VPs and thematic VPs. For example, there is a VP for the Human Development Department (which includes the global practices of education, health and nutrition, and social protection and jobs) and a VP for the Latin America and the Caribbean (LAC) region.[1] In regional development banks, like the IDB, there are more-specific subregional departments. For example, the subregional departments include Central America, the Caribbean, and the Southern Cone. In addition, there are two vice presidencies—one for "Sectors and Knowledge" and another to encompass the subregional departments.

Appendix table 1 illustrates how the World Bank's matrix works for technical sectors. The matrices of the IDB and other regional banks are similar—the only difference between the WB and regional development banks being that in the latter, what would be "regions" at the WB are instead specific subregions. For example, given its regional focus on Latin America and the Caribbean, at the IDB the subregions include the Andean countries, Brazil (the largest country and thus treated as its own subregion), the Caribbean, Mexico and Central America, and the Southern Cone countries.

The first row in appendix table 1 shows all the regions and the Global Practice units. The concept behind the matrix is that even though staff are assigned to work primarily in one region, there should ideally be knowledge sharing across regions. The Global Practice unit's main role is to promote such knowledge sharing between staff working in different regions. The first column lists all technical departments and sectors within each vice presidency. An important objective of this type of matrix organization is to capitalize on specific technical knowledge relevant to each sector, while simultaneously promoting "cross-sector collaboration"—collaboration between staff from different sectors to deliver more impactful programs and promote learning across countries.

To help bring this table to life, I have indicated in which units I worked as a YP, as well as the various positions I held (and the length of time I spent in each) during my eleven years at the WB. For example, my first YP rotation was in the Development Economics Research Group (DECRG), which is in the Development Economics vice presidency. Notice that this vice presidency does not have a regional division since all the staff there conduct data collection and research across multiple regions, or even globally. In contrast, the other four technical vice presidencies (Human Development; Sustainable Development; Equitable Growth, Finance, and Institutions; and Infrastructure), together with the regional vice presidencies, carry out the World Bank's country-based lending operations and technical assistance programs, and lead the policy dialogue with governments across the world.

As indicated in the table, my second YP rotation was in the education sector within the Middle East and North Africa region. It was during this time that I realized I wanted to work in this type of department. In contrast to my experience in DECRG, I thrived in the fast-paced, operational environment that is the bread and butter of development banks. Although I liked conducting research, I especially loved when research was at the request of an actual policymaker to inform real policymaking, as is often the case in the operational departments. After this rotation, I graduated from the YPP and began my first permanent assignment in the education sector of the LAC region.

My last position at the World Bank, shortly before leaving to join the IDB, was as HD sector leader for Central America. This position was both cross-sector and regional, and, given my decision to leave the WB, I was briefly responsible for overseeing work in the education; health, nutrition, and population; social protection and jobs; and gender sectors for the Central American region of the LAC vice presidency.

The Board

The Board of Directors (also called the Board of Governors) is technically not part of the matrix, but it is an essential component of any IDO. It is important to understand how it functions, as well as how to interact with and work alongside it, to amplify your potential impact.

IDOs generally have a Board of Directors composed of representatives from all member countries—donor countries as well as recipient, or client, countries. At present, the WB's board consists of twenty-five executive directors; the IDB's board currently has fourteen. These executive directors, and their alternates, are politically appointed by their governments and are usually former government officials (ministers, central bankers, etc.) who have technical or policy backgrounds. Their main responsibilities are to consider and decide on loan and grant proposals made by management, and to decide on the policies that guide the institutions' general operations.

Each IDO has a different distribution of ownership shares among the donor and client countries. While I was at the WB, donors (especially the United States and Japan) had a controlling majority of the shares, and thus votes. In contrast, at the IDB, the borrowing member (or client) countries had 51 percent of the votes. It is not surprising, then, that throughout Latin America and the Caribbean, the IDB was perceived as the "friendly bank," whereas the World Bank and the International Monetary Fund (IMF) were often accused of pushing the agendas of donor countries.

At the IDB, it is required for division chiefs to personally present their team's loan and large technical assistance grant proposals (the latter over a certain threshold, for example, one million US dollars) to the Board of Directors for approval. The project team leader (TL) also presents their project, but only after the introductory presentation by the division chief. The chief's role is to highlight the strategic relevance of the specific project concerning the IDB's strategy in the sector, for example in my case, education. I don't remember this being the case at the World Bank, where only exceptional projects (those that had high risks or had triggered management concerns) are presented to the board, usually by the TL.

The WB's Board of Directors usually schedules project proposal presentations on Tuesdays, and at the IDB it was always on Wednesdays. The number of project proposals depends on the time of year. At the beginning of the fiscal year, there are likely to be only a few proposals, as teams have not had much time to flesh out a new project document. At the end of the fiscal year, there are typically many projects and greater time pressure to obtain approval for all the budgeted "pipeline" projects. At the IDB, this latter period was referred to as the "bunching" period, and the executive vice president and her team did everything they could, without much success, to mitigate having too many projects presented to the board at the end of the fiscal year.

I was lucky to have a friend, the then–country director for Brazil, share some tips with me before my first presentation to the IDB board. She cautioned, "Be prepared for a tsunami. You won't know when or who, but one of the directors at some point will ask you a question that will completely throw you off-base. The trick is to keep a straight face and, no matter what, to make sure to respond to each and every one of the directors' questions."

On the Wednesday morning of my first presentation as Education Division Chief to the IDB Board of Directors in the fall of 2012, my team and I arrived promptly at exactly 8:45 a.m. in the lobby outside the boardroom. The board assistant swiped our IDs to ensure that they'd work with the microphones in the boardroom for the simultaneous interpreters. (There are always at least four interpreters, one for each of the IDB official languages—English, Spanish, Portuguese, and French. They sit in an enclosed section of the boardroom with internal windows, facing the large table so that they can observe and hear whoever is speaking.) We then sat outside the boardroom, in a living-room-style area equipped with blue sofas, chairs, and a coffee table.

There, we chatted with other division chiefs and their teams whose project presentations were also scheduled for that morning. Usually, there were two or three teams, each with three or four members, waiting outside at any given moment. Most were nervously chatting about current events, while those responsible for presenting would be focused on reviewing their talking points. Formal wear was a requirement—men wore suits and ties, and women wore skirts or pantsuits. I remember wearing a navy dress with a matching blazer, and a colorful silk scarf of birds and flowers (a gift from my sister from a recent trip to Italy) tied around my neck. I generally dressed formally for work anyway, and even more so for these types of occasions. In the more traditional IDB setting, appropriate dress makes a difference, and I find it a confidence booster.

We were second or third in line to present. The exact timing of one's presentation is always uncertain, as it depends on each team's presentation and following Q&A. Immediately after the previous team was excused, the board assistant came running up to us saying, "You're next!" We were expected to stand and wait at the doors and then enter as soon as the previous presenters exited. The message was this: don't waste a minute of the board's time.

When the double doors of the boardroom opened, the previous team emerged with smiles on their faces. Their fellow team members, who had been waiting outside, shared in congratulatory hugs. I must have lingered there watching them a second longer than I should have, as the board assistant yelled right into my face, "It's your turn! Hurry up!"

As I walked in, I saw the long wooden table in the middle of the room with four chairs on the far end where the IDB's president, executive vice president (EVP), and board secretary were seated. There were also about fifteen chairs along each side of the table where the executive directors were all seated. My team and I sat down along the side opposite the president, EVP, and board secretary. Each seat came with a microphone for simultaneous interpretation, a notepad and pencil, and a glass of water. Surrounding the centered table were auditorium-style chairs for observers to sit and listen in. These observers included the staff of the directors, president, and EVP, as well as sector managers and other IDB staff who are senior enough to attend but were not presenting. These observing officials may, and often do, intervene if the presenters or the president ask them to, or if further clarifications are necessary.

Each team is given a maximum of five minutes to make a high-level pitch for their project, and it is expected that the directors will have read the documents and are prepared with their questions. One thing I always found amusing was that even when the directors did not have any questions or comments, they still seemed somewhat compelled to speak. It therefore seems to take an unnecessarily long time to have your project discussed by the board, especially when the discussion is not productive. In most cases, by the time you present your project to the board, the chances of gaining their approval are very high because you've been through a long internal process of review and approval from different key stakeholders. (During my seven years at the IDB, I only heard of one project proposal that was not approved by the board.)

All the same, the fact that there is a high probability of your project being approved does not make the experience of presenting any less nerve-racking. You feel as though you're on trial, with the jury seated along the sides of the table and the judge, the president of the Bank (your ultimate boss), seated directly across the table from you. I developed several strategies to overcome the stress and make the process as efficient as possible.

First, I used my two to three minutes to highlight, at a very high level, why the project was going to have an impact in the country and why it was key for the Bank to be involved. I gave very few details of the project itself. For one, I expected them to know the details from reading the documentation our team had spent months preparing and passing through the Bank's bureaucracy. More importantly, I was avoiding the scenario of one of the directors picking up on some small detail to unleash the "tsunami effect," which my friend had warned me about. This strategy worked as long as I was able to make a brief presentation.

During "bunching" time—the end-of-year craze to gain approval for all planned projects—I discovered that I could become even more successful. At these times the board would sit through eight to ten presentations each week—all of which were scheduled in a single morning. They would ask the division chiefs to be as brief as possible in their remarks. When it was my turn to present a project, I decided to let them have all the time. I said, "I know you've all read our project document, and I don't need to take any of your time unnecessarily. Let's go straight to your questions and comments." Everyone, including the president of the Bank, was shocked. No other division chief had ever missed an opportunity to present to the board. Yet, I truly love efficiency and, secretly, I wanted to test how good their questions would be without having first heard a presentation. Why not begin the discussion immediately?

The president chuckled, saying something along the lines of "Well, that was indeed very efficient. Thanks, Emiliana." And I could tell that the executive directors were a bit stunned. But then, one by one, headed by the director from Japan, they each posed their questions.

In addition to the board, staff leading the technical work for sectors, such as education and health, for example, and regions (or subregions), such as East Asia and the Pacific or Latin America and the Caribbean, work closely with people from key units that provide important support services for designing and delivering programs, such as financial management, legal, and procurement services. I don't address these key services here, as they are not formally part of the "matrix." However, they play a crucial role in ensuring that projects travel successfully through all the internal approval processes, including the board presentation. I learned early on how important it is to include them as a core part of the team, especially when you are new to a country or program. A good lawyer or financial management specialist can anticipate problems and help you design projects that will have a higher probability of being implemented effectively. Moreover, their expertise is invaluable when troubleshooting unexpected issues that arise during project implementation. Therefore, they too attend board presentations of the projects in which they have been closely involved, and it is good practice to publicly acknowledge and thank them for their contributions.

INTERNAL AND INDEPENDENT EVALUATION AGENCIES

Although not formally part of the matrix, both the WB and IDB have internal and independent evaluation agencies. The internal evaluation groups report to the president and executive vice president, whereas the external evaluation agencies report directly to the board. At the WB and IDB, the internal evaluation departments are called Operations Policy and Country Services (OPCS) and Office of Strategic Planning and Development Effectiveness (SPD), respectively. The independent evaluation agency of the WB is the Independent Evaluation Group (IEG), whereas it is called the Office of Evaluation and Oversight (OVE) at the IDB.

The work of these departments is like that of an auditor, whose role is to put together the pieces of a project, conducting a thorough, ex-post assessment of how well (or not) a specific operation worked by extensively reviewing documents and interviewing key stakeholders. Many staff in these departments have previously worked in the matrix of an IDO and bring expertise from their own experiences managing operations. In addition, these agencies often recruit early career professionals with strong evaluation skills.

Note that *it is easier to move from the matrix to an IDO independent evaluation agency than to do the opposite*. The reason is that, given the nature of the "detective" work that these agencies conduct, staff there are often not appreciated by those in the matrix. In the end, we are all human. As a supervisor, I observed firsthand how those in my team, who had designed and supervised the implementation of an operation, felt a deep emotional attachment to it. So, their reaction may be understandable when, in one of these "audits," the external evaluator digs into every aspect of the completed project and finds that not everything was done in accordance to the project document. In some cases, the independent agency staff provide a detailed review of every error, unexpected event, and result not achieved or underachieved. The project staff often find themselves contesting each assertion. Then, the project staff may later be negatively inclined when they find themselves interviewing the same "auditor" as part of a recruitment panel for a role inside the matrix.

To sum up, *understanding how IDOs (and their matrix organizations) work is key for finding the job where you'll have the most impact and be the best fit.* As an early career professional, the deeper your knowledge of a specific sector, the easier it is to get your foot in the door. As your career progresses, you may aspire to remain in that sector if, like me, it is your passion. Alternatively, you may choose to branch out from a sector specialist to become a more general economist or development professional—moving from the sectors side of the matrix to the regions side. Either way, it is best to do some internal research to understand how long the leaders of the departments that interest you have been in their roles, and what the general work culture is like. The work culture across departments, and indeed the various sectors within each department, are often quite different.

How to Navigate the Matrix

Now that you understand the structure of the matrix a bit more, here are three valuable lessons I learned about how to navigate the matrix to make an impact and advance your career.

Lesson #1: Plan for your next job.

Recently, I learned that Matt Brossard was leaving his position as Chief of UNICEF's Innocenti Education Research team (READ) to move to another job within UNICEF, based in Nepal. Although I don't think I've ever met him in person, I have come to appreciate the great work Matt and his unit have produced over the years. When I received his email message announcing that the position had opened up, I replied to Matt asking where he was going to next. He replied, "Staying at UNICEF (the best org ever!!): head of education for South Asia (based in Kathmandu regional office) . . . I am leaving it now because, per UNICEF HR policy, next year is the time for my rotation and the opportunity in Kathmandu is now."[2]

Like Matt, I learned early on that planning for your next job is critical to have a fulfilling career within an IDO. During my first permanent assignment at the World Bank after graduating from the YPP, a colleague who had also been in the YPP only a few years ahead of me told me she was about to leave the education sector of the Latin America and Caribbean region, which I had just joined. I asked, "Why so soon?" She replied, "Because if I don't find myself a position that I really like, I will soon be forced to move to anything that becomes available. Make sure you start looking before it's too late!"

As explained in chapter 4, for my first permanent assignment, I took a position in the education sector in the HD Department of the LAC region. I made this decision for at least three reasons. First, I was eager to work on education issues in my region of origin. Second, I had heard through the grapevine that the newly appointed director of the HD Department in LAC was a progressive female leader who deeply promoted work-life balance and rewarded performance, not merely hours spent at work. As a mother of two young children, I needed this flexibility—to be both the mother and professional that I deeply desired to be. Third, the travel distances and time differences between Washington, DC, and LAC are the shortest among the World Bank's regions, and there were often overnight flights to South America. This would make my travel and time in the office much more manageable given my family situation.

The key lesson here is to *know your priorities* when planning for your next job. There are many jobs that become available at any given time, and you want to avoid ending up in a job that limits your potential or does not match your interests and work-life balance. Don't take a job in the wrong place for the sake of a staff position. Better to start in a consultancy in operations or research, or where your true technical interest is, and work your way in.

Another tip is to *begin by doing your research*. By this I mean you should invest in networking with people and learning about which jobs are likely to be opening up soon. Again, you should start this process during your fourth year (latest) in any given job. If you wait until years five or six, by the time you are forced to rotate (in year seven), there may be no jobs available that are a great match for you.

At the WB and other large IDOs, like the UN, you can have a long career with multiple jobs. Perhaps the most important factor to consider when looking for your next job is your future direct supervisor, and how long they have been in the job. I enjoyed the autonomy employees have at every level including the sector directors and managers. Not only do they set strategic priorities, but they also establish, for better or worse, the individual sector's unique working culture.

As I considered my next job placement, I would research how long the sector manager and director had been in their position in the department. If they had been there three or more years, they were likely to soon rotate. I intentionally chose to move to jobs where both the manager and director had recently been appointed. I therefore knew who I'd be working under for the entire time I'd be there.

Consider how long you want to stay in each role. I ended up taking a new job every four years during my time at the World Bank because good matches came up when I started networking toward the end of my third, or the beginning of my fourth, year and, like Matt Brossard, I didn't want to lose out on those opportunities. I also concluded that the first two years in a new job are when you experience the steepest learning curve. In the third and fourth years, you reach your maximum productivity point. And, since I was always eager to learn and grow even more, I was ready for a new challenge at the end of every fourth year.

Lesson #2: Your present job choices affect your future opportunities. In planning for your next job, try to gain a clear understanding of how a given position may open or close opportunities in the future. For example, you may be completing a graduate degree and have strong impact evaluation skills. The WB's Independent Evaluation Group (IEG) or the IDB's Office of Oversight and Evaluation (OVE) may have an open position, and you're likely to be a strong candidate.

My advice? If you want a long career in an IDO, do *not* start in their independent evaluation agencies. For the reasons I mentioned earlier, these agencies are the internal auditors for the organization, determining the failings of each project and documenting them extensively. Truthfully, while this is indeed their responsibility, the reality is that no project is perfectly designed or implemented exactly as it was designed on paper. Additionally, development projects seldom achieve all the expected results. Such is life.

And yet, when your IEG/OVE colleague articulates in black and white all that went wrong in a project you worked so hard on for many years, you can't help but feel affronted. Subsequently, if you're ever in a hiring position, as I was, and the person who had previously evaluated your project applies for the job, it is very difficult to think of them as a well-intentioned colleague. Over and over, I saw intelligent and committed development professionals trying to move from the independent evaluation agencies to the regular matrix. It rarely happened.

Growing into more of a development generalist than a sector specialist is also a valid strategy for navigating the matrix. In general, staff working in the country side of the matrix are development economists or generalists, who understand the basics of economic development and rely on sector experts as needed. Therefore, staff working on the sector side of the matrix are those who have a deeper understanding of their specific sector, such as education, health, or social protection. One of my good friends and former colleague from the WB's education sector is now a country representative (a position in the country side of the matrix). Like me, she earned a doctorate from a graduate school of education at an Ivy League university. Also like me, throughout the first half of her career at the WB, she managed both lending and research projects. I purposefully stayed away from the region side of the matrix because I didn't think I would enjoy it as much as continuing to work in the education sector.

In contrast, the role of country representative is something that my friend has thoroughly enjoyed. She thrives in leading negotiations with government counterparts and learning about the different development issues, as most country-side staff are required to do. It is highly unlikely that she will go back to the education sector, and, for her next rotation, she is looking into other country-representative or country-director opportunities.

My advice here is to know yourself. If you, like me, want to become an expert and have a passion for a specific sector, then it's best to stay in the sector side of the matrix. But if you, like my friend, are eager to learn more broadly about multiple sectors and enjoy the give-and-take of government negotiations, then the country side of the matrix could be a great opportunity for you.

Finally, if you move from the technical departments (sector or country side) in the matrix to the IDOs' areas of support, for example, human resources (HR), procurement, financial management, or general operations support, I can practically guarantee that you will be unable to transition back to one of the technical departments in the matrix. This is because while taking on one of these support functions, you will become much more knowledgeable about the IDO-specific policies and procedures than on technical development issues. Your more limited knowledge and experience in project implementation will likely become a disadvantage when applying for these technical positions.

Lesson #3: Follow the money.

You may be wondering who is more powerful: the country (regional vice presidencies) or the sector (Global Practice vice presidencies) side? Well, it boils down to which side controls the budgets—and this sometimes changes during reorganizations.

Currently, at the WB, the regional vice presidencies control not only the budget allocation to sectors for lending operations, but also budgets for technical assistance and applied research—called "analytical and advisory activities," or AAA.

As a sector specialist, like I was at the WB, you have one direct supervisor to whom you are mapped—your practice manager (or division chief, in the case of the IDB). At the same time, the country director (and country manager), for the countries wherein you work, has oversight and is a decision-maker. There is also a program leader who has responsibility for coordinating across sectors within the country and though not your supervisor, can be a key internal stakeholder. For example, during my first permanent assignment in the education sector of the HD Department in LAC, I reported to the education sector manager, the country director for Southern Cone countries, *and* the HD sector leader. All three of them reviewed my work and influenced which projects I was involved in, as well as when I could be promoted.

At the IDB, things are a bit different. The country side of the matrix still controls the budgets for all lending operations; however, the sector side controls the resources for technical assistance, economic, and sector work. This difference made the position of Education Division Chief at the IDB much more attractive to me than the similar position of Education Sector Manager at the WB. As the IDB's Education Division Chief, I was able to allocate *resources*, not just people, to sector priorities that I could define. In contrast, the Education Sector Manager at the WB has limited say over what technical assistance programs and applied research should take place. Instead, this is determined by the country directors in coordination with the sector leaders, and the sector manager is primarily responsible for managing the people in their team.

The bottom line: a strong understanding of how the organizational structure of an IDO works is critical to successfully navigating it for a fulfilling and impactful career. Most IDOs have a matrix structure, with sectors and regions that intersect in almost every job. To effectively navigate the matrix, first, make sure you collaborate with others, taking advantage of the expertise of colleagues to complement your knowledge and skills to enhance the impact of your work. It's also important to understand the interests of key decision-makers and how you can align or position your work to align with their interests.

Second, remember that while you remain with the same employer, there is an opportunity for you to have a series of very different jobs, spanning a long and diverse career spent within a single IDO. *Do not wait until the end of your rotation to begin looking for your next job.* Make sure to do your research and move jobs when you find the best possible fit, rather than when you have to. Think carefully about how a potential job may open or close future opportunities.

Finally, *it is key to understand who manages the budgets and people*—"money is power." When you have access to funding decisions, you can have an even greater influence on the issues you care most about.

6

All About Operations and Analytical Activities

Investment Project Financing by the Bank aims to promote poverty reduction and sustainable development of member countries by providing financial and related operational support to specific Projects that promote broad-based economic growth, contribute to social and environmental sustainability, enhance the effectiveness of the public or private sectors, or otherwise contribute to the overall development of member states.[1]

—The World Bank

In October 2007, as I was leaving Montevideo, Uruguay, to return to Washington, DC, the passport control officer at the airport recognized my name and said, "I saw you last night on the TV news. You said our education system is not of high quality. I thought we had great public schools." She was referring to the public presentation of a World Bank report titled "Education Quality and Equity in Uruguay," which I had given the day before to leaders of the National Administration of Public Education (ANEP) and about three hundred teachers. For the first time, I felt famous! With less than 3.5 million in population, Uruguay may be a small country, but the education system is of prime importance. I couldn't imagine this happening in a larger country. And hence my limited fame!

In the report, my coauthors and I presented evidence that the learning outcomes of Uruguayan students had remained stagnant for the past decade. They had been among the highest in the region ten years before, when the first round of the Programme for International Student Assessment (PISA) was conducted in 1997. Ten years later, they were comparable to the average test scores of students in other Latin American countries and well below the average of high-income, OECD (Organisation for Economic Co-operation and Development) countries. Using data from both the PISA and from national assessments, we also highlighted that educational outcomes were highly unequal, with students from low-income households scoring significantly below their peers from high-income households.

While our findings were not favorable, ANEP's leaders, who we had briefed beforehand, had organized the public dissemination of the results, and invited the media to use our findings to gain public and political support to advance major education reforms. I was nervous before the event and relieved that it had been received so well by the Uruguayan leaders. I was excited to observe how my research could be used by these policymakers as a catalyst for change. In the end, the work in IDOs is all about influencing the decision-making process in low- and middle-income countries (LMICs)—whether via research, financial support, or technical assistance.

At this point, I'd like to take your understanding beyond what IDOs do to what *you* would do as an employee of the WB or another multilateral development organization. In this chapter, I describe and categorize the different kinds of work that one could become involved with in an IDO. I also provide useful details about what one's day-to-day tasks and activities may look like, as well as how these would feed into the organization's efforts to positively impact the policies of member countries. My work has centered on the work I am most familiar with, the role of development banks. My efforts most often involved researching, advising, and funding education systems in LMICs.

Operations

Broadly speaking, there are two types of so-called operational activities (*operations*) that development banks perform. These are the design, supervision, completion, and evaluation of (a) *projects* financed via loans (lending projects)[2] and (b) *technical assistance* (*cooperation*) *programs*, or grants (which are nonreimbursable—that is, the beneficiary countries are not required to pay back the financial resources to the IDO). The key difference between the two is that the latter involve smaller grants to support either pilot projects or applied research, whereas the former are the more typical projects financed by loans from the development banks.

As someone convinced that education is the key to economic and social development, it was critical for me to ensure that the education sector would be one of the (few) sectors prioritized in each "Country Strategy." That is because these operational activities, the loans and grants, should be justified within the IDO's Country Strategy—a document that is usually prepared by the IDO staff in consultation with the client country's transition or newly elected administration, during a change in administration in the client country.

The goal of the Country Strategy is to have broad agreements on the sectors the IDO will support as soon as possible after a change in government. This ensures that the design and implementation of externally financed projects can promptly begin and continue for as long as possible and for the entire period in office. This approach is taken as many newly elected government officials wish to quickly reap the political benefits of the (sometimes) visible results of externally financed projects, such as roads, schools, and hospitals. If the strategic agreements between the political parties within a single country do not happen early on in an administrative term, it is unlikely that the political benefits will accrue to the individuals who worked on their design.

At the World Bank and Inter-American Development Bank, the Country Strategy (also referred to as the Country Partnership Framework) broadly describes a country's development progress and challenges in multiple sectors. In addition, it reviews how different IDOs have been cooperating in that country and lays out a four- or five-year cooperation strategy for the banks' overall financial and technical assistance—including loans, grants, and analytical and advisory activities as agreed upon between the incoming administration and the IDO.

As Education Division chief, having ensured that education was included in the Country Strategy allowed the client government to borrow additional funds or receive technical assistance for the sector later during their term in office. In this way, my colleagues in the region side of the IDB were more likely to support a new operation in education. It also provided me with the argument that our sector was among the priorities that were initially agreed upon in the Country Strategy. Also, the Bank's budget envelope for operations in that country was already committed to the education sector, among others. On the occasions where the education sector had not been included in the Country Strategy, a country director may decide to move forward with an education project. This was more likely to happen when another sector had not yet successfully concluded the design of a new operation and there was a risk of not meeting the agreed-upon lending portfolio within the timeline of the Country Strategy. I provided a detailed explanation of the structural divisions between regions and sectors in chapter 5, "Navigating the Matrix."

Analytical and Advisory Activities

In addition to the operational activities, IDOs carry out applied research often referred to as *economic and sector work* (ESW). ESW includes assessments of progress made to date in expanding educational opportunities, financial and human resource capacity, and constraints, as well as recommendations on how the country could progress toward raising educational outcomes for students. Examples include evaluation of pilot program impact, descriptive studies of trends in important development issues, and evaluation of economic and other sector policies in the client countries. The ultimate goal is to inform policymaking in LMICs.

These activities are funded by internal sector budgets assigned by the regions at the beginning of the fiscal year. Funds are allocated through competitive processes—either by internal resources managed by regions or by so-called trust funds, which are provided by external funders and managed by the IDO. The WB has one of the largest and most influential trust funds, the Strategic Impact Evaluation Fund (SIEF), which finances rigorous evaluations of programs and policies intended to improve development outcomes in LMICs.[3]

The "Education Quality and Equity in Uruguay" study I mentioned at the opening of this chapter is an example of this type of applied research. After the concept note (CN) I had prepared was approved, I was able to use my ESW budget to recruit other WB staff to be part of the team. It also enabled me to hire external consultants, travel to Uruguay to gather data, interview key informants, and consult with government authorities at various stages to ensure we were addressing high-priority policy issues. The final report, after it had undergone the internal peer review and approval process, was shared with the Uruguayan authorities and publicly disseminated. Our findings helped inform government-led reforms to strengthen student learning assessment systems and teacher practices.

An example of a sector diagnosis is "Argentina: Building a Skilled Labor Force for Sustained and Equitable Economic Growth: Education, Training and Labor Markets in Argentina,"[4] which I coauthored with my friend and former WB colleague Harry Patrinos. ESW may also include causal research, such as a randomized control trial (RCT) to evaluate a specific intervention designed to improve a set of competencies or skills. There are also several studies that IDOs conduct on a regular and more ongoing basis. For example, public expenditure reviews entail IDO staff analyzing a government's budget and spending within key sectors to help inform future lending operations, as well as improve the country's financing policies.

To complement country-specific research, the research departments of IDOs often conduct large-scale surveys of key development indicators in multiple countries. These surveys incorporate indicators of health and nutrition, education attainment, employment, and labor market outcomes of a representative sample of the population. The data produced are considered public goods and are made widely available not only to the IDO staff, but also to external researchers in order to promote and support high-quality research of development challenges. For example, an independent researcher investigating access to health and nutrition for children in sub-Saharan Africa benefits from comparisons to peer groups in other regions of the world. Such comparisons would be time-consuming to produce without access to the data and findings produced by IDOs.

THE PROJECT CYCLE

The operational activities (loans, grants, and technical assistance projects) take place according to a series of steps that must be completed in a specific sequence. Within multilateral development banks, such as the WB and the IDB, this is known as the *project cycle* and involves extensive documentation of project preparation and implementation through a defined set of stages (see figure 1).

The first stage in the project cycle is *identification*. This is usually in response to a client government's request for financial and/or technical assistance. The IDO staff and consultants travel to the client country to identify the main development issues that a Bank project could address (typically called a "mission"). During the mission they discuss potential costs and how these are to be shared between the external funder (WB, for example) and the government.[5] In some cases, there may be more than one external funder included in these discussions, such as another multilateral development bank, a bilateral organization, or even a philanthropic IDO.

The product of an identification mission is the project concept note (PCN), which details the main objectives and components of the proposed project and estimates the total costs and how they are to be distributed across the project components, as well as the proposed duration of the project. Once the team leader (TL) and direct supervisor(s) agree, the PCN undergoes a *peer review* process before it is formally approved by the IDO management. This is required before the TL may move to

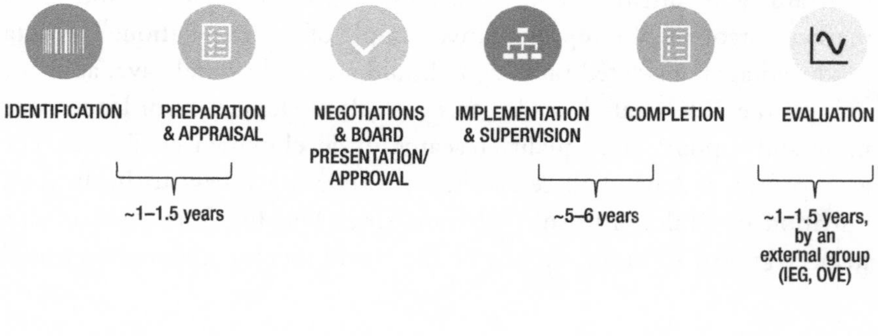

the next stage. The peer review process for the PCN (and all other project documentation) involves selecting a few colleagues and sometimes external experts with relevant expertise to provide technical feedback, in writing or in person, and holding a formal review meeting, which is usually chaired by the Bank's country director. The country director, sector manager, sector leader, TL, and peer reviewers are all present at PCN review meetings. Peer reviewers may have the option of providing written feedback beforehand if they are not able to attend in person.

The review meeting is open to others within the organization who work in related sectors for the same region or in the same sector for other regions. Everyone is encouraged to provide feedback, which is recorded in the PCN Review Meeting Minutes and then formally approval by the country director after the meeting. Once the PCN and the minutes from the review meeting are approved, the TL can progress to the project *preparation* stage.

The main goals of the project preparation stage are to advance the project design; closely collaborate with government counterparts to delineate, in detail, the project components; estimate the costs and their distribution across these components; and identify the government agencies responsible for project implementation. Project components include, for example, infrastructure, capacity strengthening, and digital technology components. In cases where government agencies are understaffed, the government and the funder may agree to establish a Project Implementation Unit (PIU) and hire additional staff to assist in project coordination. The costs of such a PIU, inclusive of staff salaries and necessary rental costs, would then be included in the total cost estimate of the loan.

Depending on the level of complexity of the project, more than one mission to the country may need to take place to work with local authorities on the project's design during the preparation stage. The TL leads the missions and invites other IDO staff and consultants to accompany them as needed. For example, an education specialist leading the preparation of a new project may need to hire engineers and/or architects to inform the infrastructure component of a loan.

The project preparation phase leads to its *appraisal*, which yields another document, prepared by the TL and project preparation team. At the WB this is called the project appraisal document (PAD); its equivalent at the IDB is the project document (PD). The PAD/PD also goes through an internal peer review process which ends in official approval by the IDO's "senior management." Once the PAD/PD has been officially approved in a review meeting and duly recorded in the minutes, the team is authorized to proceed to negotiate the final loan agreement (LA) with the government counterparts. After these negotiations are finalized and the LA has been signed by the parties' authorized representatives, the team must present the project to the Board of Directors for final approval. In total, it takes an average of about one to one and a half years to complete the identification, preparation, and appraisal stages and attain board approval.

As soon as the project has been approved by the board, the project *implementation* stage begins. As mentioned before, project implementation is the government's responsibility, therefore this stage is often referred to internally as "supervision." The responsibility of the TL now entails ensuring that the government implementers meet their commitments as described in the PD and LA or to make amendments to the LA as required, and where appropriate. The main documentation that takes place during the supervision stage is the aide-mémoire (AM, or "memory aid"), which summarizes the project's progress as evaluated by the Bank's team during their supervision mission. The project AMs collectively document the history of the project's implementation, which, on average, spans five to six years.

The next stage in the project cycle is *completion*. This stage coincides with the end date of the loan agreement, when the expectation is that all project components would have been implemented by this time, and the loan funds executed (spent) by the borrowing-country government. In collaboration with the government counterparts, the TL is responsible for preparing a project completion report (PCR). The PCR documents what the project achieved, how it was implemented, and how the resources from both the IDO and the government counterpart were employed, as well as lessons learned to inform future operations. The PCR is approved by the Bank's senior management and shared internally across the relevant sectors and regions, and duly registered in the IDO's internal information management systems.

When I was the TL responsible for supervising an education loan, designed by my predecessor, for Uruguay, one of the conditions that had been agreed upon during the preparation phase was the passing and enforcement of new legislation that would prohibit first-grade teachers from holding students back who did not achieve sufficient reading proficiency. This condition was based on evidence derived from the cognitive sciences that indicated children learn to read at different rates, and that some take longer than others. There was an emerging consensus that the grade during which children should have an adequate reading proficiency to be able to continue progressing in school was the third grade, when children are usually eight or nine years old, and not first grade, when they are only six years old.

While Uruguay's parliament passed the legislation as agreed with the World Bank, Uruguayan elementary school teachers strongly opposed it, and there was evidence that a significant share of first-grade students were still being held back from second grade. As a result, a proportion of the loan funds were being withheld by the WB from the government of Uruguay, and this was—as you can imagine—resulting in some tension between the parties. Indeed, the rest of the project activities were progressing according to plan, and the authorities argued that it was unfair to not receive the full amount of the loan because of the teachers' resistance to an externally imposed condition. As we were approaching the project completion phase, and in consultation with the WB lawyers and senior management, we decided to amend the agreement and waive this condition, which enabled the WB to disburse the remaining funds of the loan to the government and formally close the operation (and draft the PCR).

The final stage of the project cycle is *evaluation*. This is carried out by the project team after the so-called project closing when all the funds have been transferred and accounted for. Afterward, the IDO's evaluation agency (Independent Evaluation Group for the WB and Office of Evaluation for the IDB) conducts an external evaluation. These are the auditors mentioned earlier. Their role is to provide an objective assessment of the project implementation and achievements rather than rely solely on the team responsible for designing and supervising the project. While the project's TL and wider team do not lead the evaluation, they do play a critical role in providing necessary data and their own perspectives, as well as access to key informants based in the project country. The final product of the evaluation phase is the project evaluation report (PER), which is distributed among the evaluation agency, the IDO staff, and the Board of Directors. Over time PERs provide valuable lessons to improve future project design and supervision—ultimately enhancing the impact of the Bank's financial and technical assistance projects.

For economic and sector work, there are internal review processes akin to those of the operational activities. However, they usually take place in two moments: at the initial (concept) stage and during the completion stage. Like the project concept note, the TL must produce a concept note (CN) for research products, select peer reviewers, and hold a review meeting to attain approval in order to proceed. Like the PCN, the CN for ESW and other research products details the activities that would be carried out as part of the research, the composition of the team (including IDO staff and external consultants), and the total budget and its allocation across the proposed activities. Once the CN has been approved, the TL can begin using, or executing, the allocated resources for their research activities.

To sum up, IDOs support LMICs through various instruments, including grants, loans, and technical assistance. For each instrument, there are guidelines and tool kits to ensure a baseline of quality. At the same time, there is a lot of room to be creative and ambitious, and to work closely with government counterparts to develop innovative programs and interventions to improve the lives of citizens across the globe. The more you can combine instruments, for example, by conducting analytical activities in countries where you already have grants or loans, the more likely you are to develop deep relationships, and knowledge, in a particular country or region. In turn, this knowledge and the relationships on the ground are critical to have the most impact.

7
No Good Idea Goes Unfunded

Practice saying 'no' in the bathroom mirror every morning before showing up at work. And, if that doesn't work, when walking down the hallways do not make eye contact with anyone.

—Jishnu Das

Jishnu Das, a former World Bank colleague, explained to a recruit to the Young Professionals Program that to succeed at WB, it was key to learn how to say "no." He explained that because there are so many interesting projects, it was inevitable that you were going to run into someone in the halls who would then invite you to join their team that was doing something particularly interesting. The next day, you'd run into someone else and the same would happen until you became swamped with juggling too many projects and unable to deliver.

While it's no surprise that IDOs provide funding to identify, design, supervise, and evaluate its operations, less well known, and (in my view) quite valuable, is the availability of ample funding to do applied research on development issues. This is true at the World Bank and other international financial institutions, including the Inter-American Development Bank. As a result, there are not just many projects financed through loans, but also many technical assistance projects and analytical activities—more work, it seems, than there are people to do it. Hence, the importance of Jishnu's advice, which I wish I had received when I first joined the Bank as a YP!

Much of this research funding is allocated according to an internally competitive process, where staff within and across departments compete for funds to carry out innovative pilot projects and impact evaluations. Because they are only available to the institution's staff, they are much more accessible than, for example, research grants from US government agencies such as the National Institutes of Health or the Institute of Education Statistics. As one of my mentors was fond of saying, "Remember, at the WB, *no good idea goes unfunded*." I discovered this to be true.

As an early or mid-career professional, how should you navigate the plethora of opportunities within IDOs to take part in interesting projects without sacrificing quality and impact?

Juan Prawda, a lead education specialist who was my operations mentor in the Latin America and the Caribbean (LAC) education sector, had a rule of thumb. He advised me to never work on more than four projects at once. I'm not certain about four being the magic number; however, it has proved a useful ballpark. The key is to be selective and choose projects that facilitate your ability to learn and grow as an individual, deliver a quality product, and have a tangible positive impact "on the ground."

As I suggest throughout this book, it is valuable to remain connected to your field of interest by conducting applied research within that specific sector. Personally, I was most productive while working on one major research project, such as a regional study, and one or two economic and sector work (ESW) projects focusing on specific countries, as well as one or two lending projects, ideally in the same countries where I was carrying out the ESW. For example, when I worked on the ESW on Education Quality and Equity in Uruguay discussed in chapter 6, "All About Operations and Analytical Activities," I was also leading the WB's primary education project in that country. Thus, I took advantage of the supervision missions for the project to collect data and share preliminary results of the ESW with key stakeholders of the education sector in Uruguay. These consultations helped inform the research and enhance its impact.

It all began for me in the spring of 2003, when Beth King was my supervisor during my first YP rotation in the WB's Research Department.

It was then that I learned that our research proposal on teacher incentive reforms across several countries had been approved for funding. At this time, Beth had moved to the education sector within the Bank's East Asia and Pacific region, and I was just returning from maternity leave to work in the education team for the LAC region. Since most of the country case studies were in Latin America, we agreed that it made sense for me to lead the work from my new position as the education economist for LAC.

This was an exceptional opportunity to receive so early on in my career. Thanks to Beth, I had a generous budget to manage, which allowed me to invite a group of top researchers from the WB and academia to collaborate in producing various case studies, for example, evaluating teacher policy reforms, broadly defined, that had taken place in recent years throughout Latin America. I was also able to hire a competent research assistant (a recent HGSE graduate), who helped me review the literature. Another benefit of leading a large regional study was reduced operational responsibilities. This meant I spent less time traveling as compared to what was typical for staff in my position—something that was especially important to me as a young mother.

Not too long after, in 2005, I published my first book through the World Bank Press—an edited volume titled *Incentives to Improve Teaching: Lessons from Latin America.*[1] I learned three important lessons from this experience. First, *you can become the World Bank's "expert" in a subject area at a very early stage of your career* if you have been doing more research in that area than most of your colleagues. Between my dissertation's focus on teacher labor markets in Latin America and the recently published book on teacher incentives, I had suddenly become an expert on teacher policies.

Second, *delivering what you proposed within the planned timeline and budget is more often the exception instead of the rule in development institutions.* I am convinced that because I was able to produce a quality publication within budget and agreed timelines, I was quickly recognized as a top performer. With this status came an increasing set of opportunities to lead an interesting array of projects and access funding.

Third, *the required proposals for these opportunities are much less demanding than you might imagine.* There are four fundamental components required: (1) a clear statement of why the topic is important and timely, (2) the proposed methodological approach (including data sources or data collection), (3) the team composition, (4) an estimated budget, and (5) a summary work plan with timelines. All this information is to be provided in three to five pages. From this stepping stone, it was with relative ease that I was able to access multiple internal grants to lead meaningful research on education policy in Latin America.

Two years after my first book, I was able to use my next big research project, a regional study on the challenge of raising student learning outcomes in the region, to publish my second book.[2] In this book, my coauthor and I argued that in the effort to meet enrollment targets for compulsory education in Latin America, the drive to achieve universal coverage appeared to have left education quality behind. We shed light on recent advances in our understanding of the policies and programs that affect student learning. We used this work to provide policymakers in Latin America, and indeed other developing regions, tools for developing effective education policies.

During the final internal review meeting, Guillermo Perry, a brilliant macroeconomist who at the time was the WB's chief economist for the LAC region, said, "I didn't know that our region had such poor student learning outcomes. Your research also shows that countries with higher average student learning outcomes also have smaller learning gaps between students from poor and more affluent households. Latin American countries have huge levels of income inequality, and unless we improve our education systems, we will continue on this path."

I was delighted that my research was helping to inform some of the most influential economists at the World Bank and in the region. Years later, Guillermo invited me to Colombia, his country of origin, where he was leading research on policies for improving teacher effectiveness and raising student learning. As he introduced me to the audience, he said, "Everything I know about education, I learned from Emiliana." While this may be a bit of an overstatement, it was still a special moment for me to hear this kind of recognition from someone I had admired for so long.[3]

Perhaps because my research was specifically focused on the LAC region, the other regions of the Bank, which could have benefited from the evidence I was presenting, were instead focused on expanding *access* to schooling, too often without sufficient interest in actual student learning. It was not until eleven years later, in 2018, that the WB's flagship *World Development Report* recognized the problem that, despite increased access to schooling, student learning remained abysmally low in the developing world.[4] Like many large multilateral organizations, the World Bank can be very siloed.

After *Raising Student Learning in Latin America and the Caribbean: The Challenge for the 21st Century* was published in 2007, and having recently been promoted to senior education economist, I wrote a proposal for a regional study focused on early childhood development. While I was thrilled that "senior management"—a term commonly used by Bank staff to refer to those higher up on the corporate ladder who ultimately make the big decisions—had chosen this topic as a priority for the LAC region, my operations and ESW work for Chile and Uruguay was consuming a great deal of time and attention. I was unsure of how I could balance this new research study and still deliver on the programs to which I was already committed. This is a very common challenge for technical staff working in regions, and more often than not, they give up on doing research to focus on the country-based work.

As Jishnu had foreshadowed, I was beginning to feel overwhelmed by my workload. And, because I had already led two large research projects that resulted in two book publications in less than four years, and I was increasingly leading complex operations in Chile and Uruguay, I asked the Human Development (HD) Director for LAC if she could find someone else to lead the regional study on early childhood development (ECD). I was relieved when she agreed to do so.

However, a few months later, while I was on mission in Montevideo, Uruguay, I received a phone call late one night in my hotel room. It was the HD Director for LAC, asking if I could take over the regional ECD study that I had initially declined. As I learned later, the staff who had been leading the ECD study had not committed the allocated budget (i.e., had not used the budget to contract research assistance or consulting services), and were behind schedule and at risk of losing their funding. The World Bank, as with most IDOs, operates with annual budgets that run from July 1 to June 30 of the following year. Failing to assign and spend a budget means that the project loses its funding entirely. Since internal grants were competitive among sectors, it would be an embarrassment for the LAC HD sector to have to return funds to the region.

I felt I had no choice but to agree to take over the ECD study. But first, given my workload leading the Bank's operations in Chile and Uruguay (which remained unchanged), I requested additional funds to hire a coauthor to work with me to produce the study. After receiving approval, I invited a young education economist, Lucrecia Santibáñez, to join me. We had met while writing my first book, *Teacher Incentives*. I had been impressed by her strong research and communication skills and thought she would be a valuable coauthor. I also anticipated that the opportunity would help advance her own career—as publishing early on had done for mine.

The downside was that we had to work only with the few deliverables that the previous team leaders had managed to produce, and they were not up to my quality standards. Lucrecia and I worked hard to produce a decent book, which we titled *The Promise of Early Childhood Development in Latin America and the Caribbean*.[5] In the book, we built upon the growing literature indicating that early childhood development outcomes play an important role throughout a person's life, significantly affecting one's income-earning capacity and productivity, longevity, health, and cognitive ability.

First, we documented early childhood development indicators in the LAC region and explored access to early childhood development services for children of different socioeconomic backgrounds. We then reviewed recent evidence on the impact of early childhood development interventions, including in health, hygiene, nutrition, education, and poverty alleviation, around the world and within the region. In addition, we analyzed more thoroughly a selection of seven exemplar ECD programs in Latin America and the Caribbean, and distilled lessons related to their design, implementation, and institutionalization processes. The book concluded with a discussion of the challenges of scaling up ECD interventions, and presented recommendations for developing national ECD policies and programs that were most likely to be both effective and sustainable over time.

Frankly, because the raw materials with which we had to work were weak, the internal peer-review process of the Bank did not go as smoothly as it had for my two previous research studies. However, senior management recognized that I had taken over a project mid-course and that Lucrecia and I had still managed to produce a useful research-to-policy-making book.

Being a valuable team player and contributing to the broader institutional goals pays off. As it turned out, of my three books, this was the one that got the most external attention. The singer-songwriter Shakira, along with other Latin American artists, was just starting a new philanthropic foundation, ALAS (América Latina en Acción Solidaria, or Latin America in Solidarity Action), focused on improving early childhood development outcomes in Latin America. My book provided the evidence she was seeking to advocate for her foundation to focus its work on ECD, and she offered to come to the WB for our book launch event to raise public interest in the issues surrounding ECD in the region.

I am a huge Shakira fan, and I was honored and excited to meet her and work with her team on the book launch event. The night before the event, which would be taking place at the WB headquarters, Shakira's team invited me to the hotel where they were staying. We went over all the details of the event, and at the end, a member of her team asked if I would autograph the book for Shakira. It was a bit of a surreal experience to be asked to sign an autograph for a world-famous celebrity!

In summary, three takeaways to remember: First, it is generally true that no good idea goes unfunded for IDOs that provide funding to LMICs, such as development banks and large private philanthropies. The caveat is that you need an idea for a research or project that will add value. If so, you will very likely be able to access the funding to carry it out.

Second, if you deliver within the budget and projected timelines, you will be recognized and rewarded with more interesting projects and more challenging, and rewarding, settings. On the flip side, if you fail to spend your allocated budgets, you lose them. In such cases you may also lose credibility that you can deliver within a specific timeline, which will affect the types of projects you can work on thereafter.

And, finally, being a good team player pays off. While you can and should try to be selective about the projects in which you are involved, you should also contribute to your unit's, or department's, broader goals. The good news is that most of the time, your own goals will align well with those of the broader organization.

8

Globally Informed, Locally Driven

In over fifteen years that the World Bank has been working in the education sector in Chile, this is the first time you have reached out to meet with us.

—Jorge Pavez, head of the Chilean teachers' union (1996–2007)

In July 2006, then-president of Chile Michelle Bachelet announced a proposal to institute a new Superintendency of Education to regulate the use of public funds by public and private schools. It would operate similarly to the Superintendency of Banks. The Minister of Education and her staff learned about this new agency like everyone else, through the news media, and quickly got to work to assemble a team to design the agency. This team included the Under-Secretary of Education, the Director of Basic Education, the Under-Secretary of Finance, and the Director of Budgeting at the Ministry of Finance. Together they sought to identify which functions (if any) of the Ministry of Education should now move to the new superintendency. In coordination with the Ministry of Finance, they asked the World Bank to provide technical assistance.

The request for help came via email to the account of my boss, Eduardo Velez-Bustillo, in August 2006, while most of the WB staff were away on summer vacation. Eduardo forwarded the request to the manager of the Public Sector Reform team (which is now the governance sector, part of the Equitable Growth, Finance, and Institutions department shown in appendix table 1, "The World Bank's Matrix"), a separate department from Human Development and the education sector. He suggested that they should be responsible for responding and leading this new project. Fortunately, he copied me on the message, and after reading the email, I privately replied to Eduardo explaining that the proposed reforms would fundamentally transform the Chilean education system and that I thought the education sector should lead the Bank's support to the government of Chile. His response was, "Well, if you want to lead it, go ahead."

From Informing Marginal Changes to Systemic Reforms

As an economist, most of my training had been focused on improving education "at the margins," that is, bit by bit. In contrast, the government of Chile was planning to overhaul the entire institutional structure of the education system. This would *not* be a marginal change. The government asked our team to draw lessons from the institutional arrangements of high-performing education systems in other countries to inform the reform plan. Although I had never done this type of qualitative comparative research, with the benefit of the WB's resources and access, I knew that I could bring in the needed expertise. It was exciting to be involved in such a fundamental reform.

After Eduardo gave me the "go-ahead" to lead the Bank's technical assistance for the education reform in Chile, I reached out to all my networks and assembled a team of external consultants, composed of senior advisers and internal junior consultants. Without having previously met them, I reached out to Sir Michael Barber, former head of UK Prime Minister Tony Blair's Delivery Unit, as well as Joseph Olchefske, who had led quality assurance reforms for the Seattle, Washington, public school system in the United States. I was thrilled when they agreed to join the team. With the resources mobilized, I hired a consultant to assist me in conducting the research and analysis. The team helped conduct a rapid review of the institutional setup of countries that, like Chile, had a large private school sector subsidized by the government, but that, unlike Chile, were successful at producing high student learning outcomes.

We had a short timeline. President Bachelet had promised to create the new agency within the year, and in Chile (as in many other countries), any such change needed to be approved by the legislative branch of the government. At the World Bank, as I explained in chapter 6, "All About Operations and Analytical Activities," any economic and sector work (ESW) must first gain approval through several stages of peer review. We had to move fast to at a minimum produce a framework and the initial dataset on the structure of the organization of the institutions in comparable countries to usefully inform the government of Chile.

In addition, I did not think it appropriate to produce a report for the Chilean government while based solely in Washington, DC, and informed only by global evidence. Besides bringing to bear lessons learned from other countries across the globe, it was important to understand the concerns and priorities of the main local stakeholders and to produce recommendations that would have the highest possible chance of being adopted. Because holding consultations with key stakeholders, including representatives from all government branches, was so crucial during this period, I traveled to Chile a couple days every month throughout 2008. Fortunately, the flights from DC to the Southern Cone countries take place overnight, making for efficient travel.

I recall one particularly exciting (and exhausting) mission during which I made the same presentation at least four times per day, for five days, to various stakeholders. Among them were the Minister of Finance, the Senate Commission on Education, the Association of Private Schools, student leaders, teachers' unions, thought leaders, and mayors of various cities. By Friday midday, I had completely lost my voice.

Among the many memorable meetings during that mission, two stand out. One was with the Colegio de Profesores—the Chilean teachers' union. My team, consisting of an external consultant, a junior consultant, and myself, arrived at their offices and were greeted by the union's president along with ten of its most senior leaders. The president welcomed us by saying, "In over fifteen years that the World Bank has been working in the education sector in Chile, this is the first time you have reached out to meet with us."

I was taken aback but quickly rebounded, saying, "Well, I apologize for this. As you can tell, the WB has also evolved quite a lot during this time. I imagine that you did not expect the WB to look like me," while pointing to myself, a relatively young Latina woman. I hoped that my relatability would win them over to listen to my presentation. They did, and a productive discussion followed. Their valuable insights were incorporated into our framework and analysis.

Another memorable meeting was with members of the Chilean Parliament's Education Commission. We had a highly effective slide illustrating what we had learned from comparing how governments around the world intervene in their education systems. They included four categories ranging from examples of "Limited State" intervention on one end of the axis to "Direct State Control" on the other end. In each of these four categories, we included the names of example countries. As I was explaining the slide, a congressman representing the right-wing party amused us all by exclaiming, "Wait, but you have the graph reversed. 'Limited State' should be on the right, and 'Direct State Control' on the left." I quickly responded, "Sir, with all due respect, we are describing our research findings, not presenting them according to ideological perspectives."

At the end of the mission, we shared the feedback from local stakeholders with Chile's Ministers of Education and Finance and their teams. We told them that while there was broad agreement on the need for institutional reform, the key stakeholders were very divided as to what extent the government should be involved in assuring education quality.

We learned that the main stakeholders had vastly different beliefs, or ideologies, about the government's role in education. Some argued for "the right to teach," meaning, in Chilean lingo, that schools should have the right to select their own learning goals, as well as their students. In contrast, others from "the left" argued that all children had the right to receive the same quality of education, regardless of their background characteristics, and that it is the government's responsibility to make this a reality. These "left" stakeholders also believed that schools should not be allowed to select their students. In the end, partly due to the evidence from other education systems across the world, the latter prevailed and the law allowing schools to select students was eventually overturned. In its place, a centralized lottery admission system was introduced, whereby families can rank their choice of schools and an algorithm matches students to schools, thereby ensuring that all students would have an equal chance of getting into a top-choice school. Indeed, the lessons from high-performing education systems, that also had a large private school sector financed by the government, were well received by all parties. These takeaways eventually became part of the key components of Chile's education quality assurance reforms adopted between 2010 and 2018.

When we were about to leave Santiago, my counterpart—the Under-Secretary of Education—made a comment that surprised me. He explained that the WB and the Inter-American Development Bank (where I would later work) operated very differently. He said, "You really get involved in the issues and do the work, whereas the IDB folks brought us a British expert who gave a conference. Then, they transcribed the speech, and it became their report."

I learned later that it is not fully accurate to state that the IDB and the WB as organizations worked differently. Rather, the respective team leaders assigned to Chile worked very differently; as a result, their relationships with the country counterparts and, ultimately, their impact was markedly different. Indeed, our work helped inform the proposed law that was approved by the Chilean Parliament in 2010 and was used to create a new Education Quality Assurance System. When I showed Eduardo the approved law, he said, "Well, if that's not *impact*, then what is?"

Throughout my career in IDOs, I was fortunate to work with economists and sector specialists who genuinely and deeply engaged with the issues they were tackling. On the other hand, I also crossed paths with others who would hire consultants to take care of the substantive work. I call the latter group the "full-fledged international development bureaucrats." They spend most of their time compiling documents, prepared by teams of more junior staff and external consultants, for approval through the various stages of the internal bureaucracy. I like to think that early in their careers they had been passionate about development issues and effecting change. Now, however, they had become, more than anything, experts at pushing paper and, in some cases, full-fledged bureaucrats.

While they helped get projects through the many stages of the project cycle, they were less concerned about potential impact. It was not necessarily all their fault; as one of my former WB colleagues put it, "Management opens champagne bottles to celebrate when a loan gets approved by the board, not when a research study is published."

Regardless of the internal rewards, I was always more fulfilled by generating evidence and advising policymakers than by getting an additional project approved by the board. I found it deeply rewarding to engage with local stakeholders and understand what would be, in their views, the most beneficial outcomes for their populations. I needed to understand the cultural and social values that would make different interventions impactful and sustainable. As a person from the so-called Global South myself who happened to live and work in the Global North, I did not deem it appropriate to decide what is best for any country. My role, as an IDO official, was to evidence from other countries that had achieved the outcomes they were seeking for their peoples and, together, to determine approaches that may be effective within their own contexts.

Figuring Out Whether a Specific IDO Is a Good Fit

A few years after my mission to Santiago with the WB, I went on a mission to Panama, my first as Education Division Chief of the IDB. Gina Montiel, the IDB's country director for Central America at the time, asked me to travel to Panama City to participate in a high-stakes meeting with the Minister of Education. Two or three years before I came on board, the IDB had approved a large loan to finance the construction of new comprehensive (K–12) schools in remote and rural areas of the country. The project's implementation, however, had become riddled with escalating prices due to a construction boom in the country, as well as pervasive corruption. Out of the six large schools that had been planned, only two had begun construction, and only one had been completed and recently inaugurated by the minister.

I met Gina at the IDB office early one morning, where her driver was waiting to take us to the Ministry of Education. John,[1] the IDB's education specialist based in Panama and who reported to me, joined us.

He was a mild-mannered US citizen, with a PhD in education from an Ivy League institution, and a fluent Spanish speaker.

The then–Minister of Education was a tall, strong woman who previously had been a prominent journalist. She was known to be a tough person. I was called on to establish a good working relationship with her to address the project's problematic implementation issues. Funnily enough, Gina explained to me that the minister would "love" me because she and I both liked to dress well! Though not related to our dress, she was right. The minister and I connected well and were able to reach some agreements on how to move the project forward. Meanwhile, John remained silent throughout the meeting, and I noticed that his face was unusually red. After we concluded the conversation and shook hands, John was the first to leave the minister's office.

As Gina and I were saying our good-byes, the minister turned to me and said, "I love that gringo of yours.[2] He gets so scared around me!" I smiled politely, but inside I was dismayed. Her comment was demeaning to John and signaled an issue I would have to address if we wanted to move forward with effective implementation. I needed John to have productive conversations with the minister or our education work in Panama might be in jeopardy.

The next day, we met with a key consultant, an engineer whom John had hired to oversee the construction of the school buildings. I asked the engineer to take me to the school that had been recently inaugurated, which, while located in a rural area, was only one hour away from the city. Schools had been closed that week due to electricity rationing, which I learned often happens in Panama. Fortunately, we were able to ask the custodian to unlock the building and a few of the classrooms. I vividly remember seeing some obvious signs of faulty construction, including cement gutters next to the playground, which I pointed out to John and the engineer. I then walked into an eighth-grade classroom, where the teacher had left a lesson on the chalkboard. Though I am no expert in curriculum development, I had an eighth-grader of my own back at home, and I was somewhat familiar with what he had been learning in school. What was on the blackboard in this classroom was content that my son had learned in fourth or fifth grade. I quietly mentioned this to John.

During that school visit, I realized that although the school was only an hour's drive from the city where John was living full-time, this was probably his first time visiting it. If the Minister of Education's comment about John had been cause for concern, I was now truly worried. John was not doing the work as I had assumed. In order to have the impact the country so badly needed, I knew I was going to have to engage in conversations to better understand John's skills and career goals. I tell you that story in chapter 13.

What were the main takeaways from my time working in Chile and Panama?

First, *policymakers can learn a great deal from the experiences of other countries and contexts.* IDOs are best placed to help make these global connections and provide lessons learned. The key to having credible results is to stay up to date on the best evidence from around the world, maintain strong networks with experts in your field, and, at the same time, connect effectively with your country counterparts. As an IDO professional, you'll be most impactful when adapting these lessons into the context relevant to local stakeholders. I was never afraid to reach out to experts whom I had not previously met and, most of the time, they agreed to collaborate with me, even when I was very young. They too deeply cared about development issues and, as an IDO staff leading work to address challenging development problems, they were often surprisingly eager to get involved.

Second, *do not be afraid to tackle the most difficult development questions.* As an economist who primarily did quantitative analyses, I had not previously conducted qualitative comparative policy analysis. Yet, it wasn't difficult to see that the president's announcement to introduce a new central government agency to complement the Ministry of Education in Chile had enormous potential for impact. If I had been too concerned about not having prior experience in qualitative comparative policy analysis, I would not have become involved in the education governance reform in

Chile. This turn out to be one of the most significant institutional country education reforms to take place in recent years.

My LAC supervisor at the WB, Eduardo, later told me that I have no fear. I realize now that having no (or little) fear of tackling seemingly impossible challenges has enabled me to continue to grow professionally and for my work to have an impact. Had I not embraced the challenge of advising the government of Chile in its reform of the national education institutions, I would not have gained valuable skills that I used later in my career to develop a global framework to analyze education policies, the Systems Approach to Better Education Results, SABER, project (which I discuss in chapter 10, "Moving Up the Corporate Ladder").

Of course, I am not suggesting that you take on challenges that you're clearly not prepared for. But, in most IDOs, there are plenty of resources (financial as well as human) that you can tap into to complement and leverage your skills. Don't say "no" to a challenging situation that has the potential to have a great impact. Instead, lean into your own as well as the myriad available resources at your disposal. You will not regret it!

Third, to produce the best work possible, *you'll need to tap into all your assets*. I learned early on that my language and cultural background were especially helpful in certain settings. I could understand the unspoken codes, and I could leverage my cultural and linguistic knowledge to build trust and stronger working relationships. Some of my former colleagues had a wonderful sense of humor, which helped them connect with people of various backgrounds to generate effective working relationships. Whatever is your "superpower," the sooner you can identify it and tap into it, the more effective you can be.

Fourth, *get involved*! Consult *all* the key local stakeholders to gain a deep and holistic understanding of their concerns and context. In Chile and Panama, my team and I consulted a wide range of stakeholders, including politicians in the executive and legislative branches, teachers' unions, parent organizations, private school owner organizations, secondary school and university student organizations, locally elected mayors, academics, and other thought leaders. Remember that as someone working in an IDO, you should bring the best global evidence. At the same time, local knowledge is just as important to inform policies to truly have an impact.

Finally, *avoid letting others (particularly external consultants) do the legwork for you.* It is important to "get your hands dirty." Make sure to travel to places where the final product of your work is located—be it schools, hospitals, or roads, for example. The insights you gain from directly observing what is happening on the ground and talking to the direct (and indirect) beneficiaries of IDO projects are invaluable. Don't allow others do the interesting work while you only synthesize information and push the work of others through the internal bureaucracies.

9

Team Player, Team Leader

You know how to play one instrument, perhaps the violin. But your role as a team leader is not to play an instrument. It is to imagine the concert, how each instrument needs to sound, and to lead all the musicians in playing that vision of the music.

—Juan Prawda

My first assignment after the YPP was in the LAC region's education team. I was assigned to projects led by Juan Prawda, who was a senior education specialist nearing retirement. The projects were in the Southern Cone countries (Argentina, Chile, and Uruguay). Our supervisors had asked him to be my operations mentor—to show me the ins and outs of managing lending operations and technical assistance projects. Initially, I was the economist responsible for applying economics and statistical analysis to inform the projects led by Juan. Over time, thanks to Juan's mentorship, I came to understand all project components and met the key counterparts and stakeholders, and I learned a great deal about the World Bank's lending operations (loans) and technical assistance (grants).

Juan, a Mexican national, had been a former Director of Planning and Budget at the Mexican Secretariat of Public Education. An engineer by training, he was extremely organized and systematic in how he planned and delivered his work. Juan is probably the only person I've ever worked with who literally scheduled all his travel plans a whole year in advance.

When I found out in September 2003 that he had scheduled a mission to Chile in which I was expected to participate during my birthday in October 2004, I politely asked if we could reschedule it to the week either before or after. His answer was a classic Juan response: "Oh, I can't change anything in my schedule at this point; it will mess up my entire year. We'll have a nice dinner to celebrate your birthday in Santiago."

He was also a very generous mentor who taught me how to take full advantage of the Bank's resources to support team leaders (TLs). While we were on a supervision mission in La Plata, Argentina (for the same project I had worked on as a summer intern), the project manager, our counterpart from the provincial government, asked us a very specific procurement question. Juan thought he knew the answer, but he still made a telephone call to our assigned procurement specialist at the WB's headquarters in Washington, DC, for verification. After confirming the correct answer and hanging up, he turned to me and said, "You see, Emiliana, you do not need to know everything about operations. You just need to contact the staff who know, and you'll always give the client the right advice and stay out of trouble."

This was some of the best advice I received about leading operations. It allowed me to focus on what I like most—the technical aspects of the project, such as the theory of change and how the activities would lead to improved outcomes for students. It also allowed me to leave all the operational details to other team members whose expertise and responsibility were to focus on those aspects. This included financial management and procurement, which are critical for a project's success but were not part of my training—and, frankly, were not of great interest. While these skills can be very helpful within specific IDOs, they are not easily transferable to other institutions, including organizations in the private sector and academia. Instead, I chose to spend my time developing the skills that would be valuable not only within the confines of a single organization but also outside. As a result, I always had flexibility and options, which has led to a very fulfilling career.

Team Leader Autonomy: A Double-Edged Sword

During my first year in the LAC education sector of the WB, I learned that team leaders have a great deal of autonomy in how they conduct the Bank's business. Juan set the mission dates, defined the mission team members (including hiring consultants when he thought necessary), and worked with the counterparts from member countries to define mission agendas. While on a mission, he always scheduled appointments for lunch or dinner with experts outside of the WB. These included former government officials or policy analysts who could offer us an insider's perspective of the political and policy environments that as an outsider was difficult to gauge. After traveling on a few missions with Juan, I began to do the same. As a result, I gradually grew my own network of experts from the region whom I could trust for honest advice and feedback—many of whom I have continued to collaborate with over the years.

In October 2004, Joel Reyes, a colleague working in the Central America region, accompanied us on our mission to Chile—that had, of course, been planned a whole year prior. The Bank had been encouraging and investing in staff shadowing each other's missions to learn and exchange best practices. Joel was soft-spoken with a gentle temperament, and so very different from Juan's hyper-organized, direct, and unapologetic way of managing operations.

This was a supervision mission for the project Chile Califica—an innovative program co-led by the Ministries of Economy, Labor, and Education of Chile, and for which the Bank had approved a six-year loan under Juan's leadership. The project aimed to strengthen the technical-vocational education and training offerings, linked to the country's economic development strategy as well as the demands of the private sector.

There were many units across various agencies involved in carrying out a myriad of project components and activities—ranging from providing adult literacy education (led by the Ministry of Education) and building "one-stop shops" for linking unemployed individuals to training and job opportunities (led by the Ministry of Labor), to crafting a new national skills certification system (led by Fundación Chile, a nonprofit, public-private organization charged with promoting innovation in Chile). The project had an Advisory Council, which was chaired by the Minister of the Economy and was composed of the Ministers of Education and Labor, and also included the president of Fundación Chile. There was also a Project Implementation Unit, staffed with a director and a small team who were responsible for managing the loan and reporting the project's progress and challenges to the Bank.

As usual with Juan, the mission agenda was packed with back-to-back meetings with our counterparts, the directors, and their teams in the project's various implementation units (departments within government agencies across the various ministries that were responsible for leading the implementation in the country). He made sure to get a full report on each project component and subcomponent and to have ample time to dive deeper into areas that needed more of his, and the team's, attention. It was overwhelming at first, but over the coming months I learned to focus on gaining a deeper understanding of the project's most important activities—the ones with greatest impact potential, and aspects that were receiving the most funding.

Every evening after we had concluded our day of meetings with the government counterparts, the Bank's team would work on the aide-mémoire (AM). Juan always reserved at least two hours toward the end of the mission to review the draft AM with our project counterparts. This ensured that they could also contribute to the AM, which would be later shared with their own Ministries of Education and Finance and become part of the WB's official operational records.

One morning on this mission, after two meetings with various implementing units, Ignacio, the Chile Califica project director, asked Joel an interesting question: "How does the Bank work in Central America?" Joel's answer surprised me. He said, "You know, Ignacio, here in Chile the Bank is Juan Prawda. He decides how the Bank works and that is the country's experience. In Central America, the Bank is Joel Reyes. Hence, the Bank works differently depending on who the team leader is."

I found Joel's answer surprisingly honest as, in my short time working in operations, I had witnessed firsthand that team leaders had immense autonomy. This surely had personal appeal and pragmatic benefits. However, it was also deeply troubling, as I had assumed that a well-funded, highly technical multilateral organization would be much more consistent in how it operated with its client countries.

Shortly thereafter, my worst fears were confirmed. Eduardo had asked me to take over the Bank's education portfolio in Uruguay from another senior specialist in the LAC education sector, whom I will call Roberto. As in most of Latin America, Uruguayan schools operated in two, sometimes three, shifts. For example, students would attend their lessons either in the morning, afternoon, or evening to allow for a single school to accommodate more students. This is largely a result of the huge and rapid expansion in access to primary and secondary education. Prior to my involvement, the Uruguayan government had taken a loan from the World Bank to move away from the schedule of multiple shifts, and instead expand a full-time school model in disadvantaged areas throughout the country. The Bank's loan included an infrastructure component to build new schools that could accommodate an entire (six- to seven-hour) school day, project-based learning, and, in some schools, a bilingual approach to learning in either Spanish and English or Spanish and Portuguese.

I only went on a single "handover" mission with Roberto, during which he was expected to transfer the responsibility of team leader to me. In stark contrast to Juan's approach, who directly participated in all mission meetings related to a project's progress, I discovered that Roberto sent his international consultants to these meetings. Of course, I accompanied the consultants during this handover mission, and together we would brief Roberto on the project's progress later each evening. The consultants drafted the AM, which Roberto signed and sent to the government authorities, who would countersign it and then send it to the project implementation unit director. His team leadership style was completely different from Juan's. While Juan was attentive to every detail of the project, including how implementation was progressing, and directly involved in every supervision meeting and briefing with government authorities, Roberto delegated most of this work to team members and consultants. As I was soon to learn, the government counterparts understood all too well who was really vested in the success of the project, and who was not.

During the following mission, my first one as TL of the Full-Time Schools project for Uruguay, I asked to visit some of the project-financed schools. We selected a school outside the capital, Montevideo, in a poor, rural area. The school was one of the bilingual Spanish-English schools. I was struck by the high quality of the infrastructure; the school building was made of sturdy red bricks, with large windows for ample fresh air. The classrooms were beautiful, as were the offices for the teaching staff and a large playground filled with equipment for children to safely play.

Feeling impressed and optimistic, the mission team and I walked into a third-grade classroom. The teacher had written the chorus for the song "Yellow Submarine" by the Beatles on the blackboard. She played the song from a cassette player while children sitting in rows of desks sang along. The young children looked smart and official in their traditional uniforms—a white collared shirt with a navy blue scarf tied in a big bow at the center, and navy blue shorts, skirts, or trousers. In relation to the impressive school facilities, I was disappointed by the pedagogy, as it was not a great example of active learning. I thought to myself, "At least the children appeared to be having fun singing in English."

The visitors included the WB's operations analyst, the project director, the head teacher, and me. The teacher whose classroom we had just entered stopped playing the song from the cassette tape and waved her hands to signal to the students that it was time to stop singing. Then, the head teacher introduced us to her students. I was standing close to a few of them and said to one, "Hi, I am Emiliana, what is your name?" The child looked at me with a puzzled expression and said nothing. I then approached a second child and asked, "Hi, how old are you?" I received a blank stare. The project director, Marina, intervened, saying in Spanish, "*No entienden* [do you not understand]?" Both kids shook their heads. I asked the head teacher and Marina whether these were new students or if they had been attending this bilingual school for some time. They explained that the school had opened three years ago, and that these students had been there since its opening—since they were in first grade!

After our classroom visits, we gathered in the teacher meeting room to debrief. Marina asked, "How is it possible that the children in third grade cannot understand even basic questions in English, such as 'what is your name'?" At first, the head teacher didn't give us a satisfying answer—suggesting instead that the students could have just been distracted. However, after some probing from my counterpart, she responded, "Marina, don't you see our surroundings? Do you think these poor children are ever going to be able to speak English?"

Back in the hotel that evening, I could barely sleep. I was sad, frustrated, and angry. I was sad that, despite the investments in school infrastructure and learning facilities, these children did not have the opportunity to learn a valuable skill—proficiency in the English language. I was frustrated that the Bank's project was not achieving its objectives of providing quality bilingual education to underserved communities. I was also angry that, despite the government's efforts, the teachers fundamentally did not *believe* that poor children were capable of learning English. This bilingual school was completely different from my own experience at Jefferson Academy, where our teachers believed that *all* of us students were capable of learning English and other subjects. I learned an important lesson in Uruguay during that mission: no matter how well designed and resourced a project is, if the key people on the front lines do not believe in its objectives and potential, the project's chance of succeeding is severely diminished.

I decided it was important to include what I had observed during those school observations in the aide-mémoire to pressure the project leadership to work harder on training teachers, with the hope of impacting their pessimistic mindsets. Just as Juan had always done, I reserved two hours toward the end of the mission to review the draft AM with the counterparts, including Marina and her team. Instead of objecting to documenting the team's key observations and recommendations, which could have reflected poorly on her as director of the Project Implementation Unit, Marina, who was as committed as any project director I ever worked with, agreed to include them in the AM.

When Marina, the Bank team, and I met with the authorities from Uruguay's National Public Education Administration, I debriefed them on the results of the supervision mission. We discussed the alarming finding that some teachers working with socioeconomically disadvantaged children in the newly built schools did not fundamentally believe these children were capable of learning English. Jointly, we decided to shift the curriculum of ongoing professional development programs to focus on addressing teacher mindsets and their expectations of students.

At the end of the meeting, Marina shared with the authorities, "I want to thank Emiliana for the way she led this mission. In my time directing this project, I have never seen such professionalism in the way World Bank missions are carried out." I was not sure what Marina was referring to, so as soon as we left the National Public Education Administration building, I asked her to explain. She told me that Roberto had never shown that he cared about the project's progress. He had never attended any of the supervision mission meetings or school visits and instead held private meetings with only a handful of powerful stakeholders, usually politicians and other senior leaders. Marina had never been consulted before regarding the AM, nor invited to participate in the closing meeting with the authorities.

Indeed, the professional autonomy that team leaders enjoy in most IDOs is a double-edged sword. I observed the same issues later at the IDB, as well as in other IDOs with which I have worked alongside. When the TL is capable and committed, remarkable things can happen. Sadly, the opposite is also true. I felt deeply disturbed by this and, in the hope of mitigating the risk of team leaders adopting an inappropriate approach to their work, during my next assignment, I joined the WB's Global Practice to help strengthen the Bank's knowledge-sharing capacity. Through this process we developed tools to support and share the work of team leaders in the education sector across all regions. (I discuss one of these efforts, the Systems Approach to Better Education Results, or SABER, in chapter 10, "Moving Up the Corporate Ladder.")

In the meantime, I took advantage of this professional autonomy myself to gather the best possible evidence to inform the loans and technical assistance projects that I had the privilege of leading. I chose to adopt Juan's team leadership style because I felt it was more respectful toward my counterparts, and it allowed me to truly understand the project's implementation. It also allowed me to directly address any issues, as opposed to relying on the consultants to make these important decisions.

For example, after Juan Prawda's retirement, I became the TL of the Chile Califica project. On my first mission in this role, I held all the required meetings and compiled detailed reports on how all the various project components were progressing. At the end of the mission, it was customary to meet with the Minister of Education to discuss the Bank's supervision mission findings and to address any pending issues. Just as Juan had taught me, I invited Ignacio, the project director, to join in on the meeting with the minister. The project was progressing satisfactorily, and there were few issues to address. About ten minutes into the meeting, I turned to the minister and asked, "What are *your* main concerns about the education system, and how could the Bank be most helpful to you?" We then talked for another hour about the policies he was trying to pass through Congress. I left the room with a fresh list of empirical questions for our research, knowing also that now we would be addressing some of the minister's most pressing concerns.

Upon leaving the Minister of Education's office, once again like Juan always had, I asked Ignacio, "How did I do?" He replied, "Okay. But you hardly talked about the project, instead focusing on your research." I explained that the reason I did not spend much time discussing the project was in great measure due to how well it was being led and implemented. I added that we had the opportunity to take advantage of some of the time with the minister to ask about his main preoccupations related to the education system in Chile. From then on, during my work in Chile, Uruguay, and all the other LAC countries, I took advantage of my team leader autonomy to discuss broader policy questions with high-level authorities. This approach led to a research agenda that could inform real policy decision-making.

While the World Bank's loans are an important instrument for providing financial resources to low- and middle-income countries, I am convinced that providing decision-makers with the information and evidence they need to make sound policy decisions is perhaps the most important role of the IDOs. The financial resources are useful and necessary to address short-term budgetary constraints, such as building or improving school infrastructure. However, it is the technical advice that IDOs are in a position to provide that can help governments design and successfully carry out programs and reforms that will turn these financial investments into the medium- and long-term impact we were working toward.

As a young professional in an IDO, how can you become a team leader and leverage this position to make a lasting impact?

When you join the WB as a Young Professional or a sectoral economist/specialist, it will take at least a year for you to be offered a leadership role for a project. This is because senior staff and management want to make sure that you are ready—not only in terms of the necessary technical skills and sectoral knowledge, but also with regard to the project management and legal responsibilities that come with the role of team leader. While not everyone is so fortunate to be assigned a mentor like Juan, everyone has access to mentor-like guidance and support from at least one TL.

At first, you may be assigned to a team to fulfill a very specific or narrow role. For example, as a YP, I was usually the "economist" on a lending project team. This meant that I was primarily responsible for conducting the economic analyses required during project preparation and supervision. Some TLs tend to pigeonhole early career professionals and consultants into these specific roles, while other TLs, like Juan, invite all team members to participate in all meetings—even if they are not directly involved in the specific issue. My suggestion is to seek out the latter type of TL whenever possible, so that you start learning sooner rather than later about all the different aspects of project management.

The most successful TLs are those who create an inclusive team environment, where all the members of the team know what is going on. Too many times I came across TLs who only shared fragments of information about the project with each of their team members, rather than ensuring that each member had a complete and thorough understanding of the project in its entirety. It took me a while to understand that by withholding information leaders could have more control over their projects, since their team members are unable to hold them fully accountable. When TLs share information widely everyone becomes eligible to contribute, and as the TL you will draw out the best attributes and skills of every team member. This is a powerful way to create ownership of the objectives across the team.

So, if you become a TL, be sure to remain open and inclusive in sharing information with all your team members—don't miss out on the great ideas and solutions they may be able to offer. Not only do you reduce interpersonal conflict and drama within the team, but it is more fun. Including all members means nobody feels left out, and it also enhances the quality and impact of the final project outcomes.

I hope that by describing the contrast between Juan's and Roberto's style of team leadership in this chapter, you will be inspired to become a truly effective TL by working closely with your project counterparts—those who are actually responsible for implementing the project in their own country. Conduct your own analysis of the progress and impact of the projects under your care, while also consulting with team members and gathering their inputs. This will only complement your own emerging conclusions. Make it a priority to provide quality, evidence-based technical advice to your counterparts and other government authorities.

As Juan had told me, a team leader is like the conductor of an orchestra, and each musician is an expert in their own instrument. As the conductor, you need to have a thorough knowledge of the overall vision and carry it through. Don't let each team member do their own thing without regularly receiving your guidance and feedback. At the same time, understand that you cannot be an expert at everything. Rely on your fellow team members to complement your own unique skills and expertise.

10

Moving Up the Corporate Ladder

Some IDO staff are wholly fulfilled remaining in the technical track throughout their careers. My mentor Juan was one of them. He loved the operational work in countries outside the United States so much that when he retired, after a mandatory "cooling-off" period (about a year in which World Bank retirees are banned from being hired as external consultants), he became an independent consultant and has been working with WB and Inter-American Development Bank education teams ever since. (Indeed, it is common for retirees to offer their services to IDOs as external consultants after they retire, and this allows current IDO staff to tap into their deep expertise.)

I am not wired that way. Though I enjoyed the operational work, I was also ambitious in wanting to be promoted up the corporate ladder. During my third year in the WB's Latin America and Caribbean region, I was promoted to Senior Education Economist. During my fourth, I began thinking about where I should go next. I believed that climbing the corporate ladder and becoming, for example, a sector manager would give me the opportunity to have even greater impact on various lending and technical assistance operations than as a team leader.

What does it take to move from the technical track to more senior management positions? And why should you even aspire to move up the corporate ladder?

In my view, the answers to these questions depend on many factors. I previously referred to one's unique "wiring," as well as personal preferences and priorities. It also depends on the internal dynamics of the specific IDO you are working for in terms of what it takes to be promoted up the management ranks. This will vary not only across IDOs, but also within a single IDO as it evolves over time. In this chapter, I share the good, the bad, and the ugly with regard to moving up the corporate ladder.

As discussed in chapter 3, "Standing Out from the Crowd," in both of the development banks where I spent most of my early career, one would likely first enter as a Young Professional, or sector economist, or even a sector specialist. Sector economists and specialists are similar in grade and career prospects. And, while YPs share the same grade level, they tend to have better opportunities to advance in the corporate ladder. Nevertheless, all three are the entry-level positions for individuals, usually in their early to mid-thirties, who have an advanced degree (master's or PhD, the latter being the preferred) and at least five years of relevant experience (for example, in an IDO, academia, or a government agency in their country of origin).

If you have fewer years of education and work experience, you may enter as a research "associate" or even "assistant." These tend to be short-term positions to support specific lending, technical assistance, or research projects, and they are less competitive than the longer-term staff positions. However, moving from these positions to an entry-level staff position is very difficult, if not impossible. Research support systems are targeted to junior professionals who may benefit from a few years of experience in an IDO before moving on to pursue advanced degrees or other career pathways.

During the YP orientation at the WB, the human resources office informed us that most technical staff only receive a single promotion throughout their entire career. The most common exception is among the YPs, who tend to be promoted more than once and reach higher levels in the corporate hierarchy. In my eleven years at the World Bank, I had the good fortune to progress through several levels. After graduating from the two-year YPP in 2003, I served as Education Economist (until 2005), Senior Education Economist (until 2011), Lead Education Economist (until 2012), and very briefly Human Development Sector Leader for

Central America before moving to the IDB as Education Division Chief in September 2012.

Unlike a YP, if you entered the WB as an economist or sector specialist (for example, an education specialist), by the time you retire, you would likely have only been promoted once to *senior* economist or *senior* sector specialist. Alternatively, if you had joined later in your career as a senior specialist, as my mentor Juan did in the education sector, you may retire having been promoted to *lead* sector specialist.

While the various levels of sector specialists are all technical positions, you may also aspire to enter the management track. In this track, there are managerial positions both in the country and the sector side. As discussed in chapter 5, those in managerial positions are the heads of sectors and departments, and vice presidencies. On the country side, you could become a country representative for a single country, a country director for a group of countries, or a regional vice president for one of the regions. These positions are ideal for those interested in working across sectors instead of, like me, in a specific sector (education). On the sector side, you could be a sector manager, a department director, or a department vice president. As you advance from sector manager to department director and vice president, you will work with a more diverse portfolio of sectors. For example, an Education Sector Manager who then rises to Human Development Director will go from only overseeing the WB's work in the education sector in a specific region to being responsible for the WB's work in education; health, nutrition, and population; social protection and jobs; and gender.

In table 2, I describe the job positions in both the technical and managerial tracks, from lower to higher levels in the corporate hierarchy. The key to moving up the corporate ladder is to figure out which are the technical and technical managerial tracks within each IDO, which is not too difficult, and then to understand how your own skills and preferences may align to them. The UN and its affiliated agencies have similar career tracks.

In the IDOs where I worked, there were fixed caps on how many *lead* specialists could be in any given sector of the entire institution. Also, as you can imagine, because there is a limited number of these positions, the

Table 2: Illustration of Job Levels by Technical and Managerial Tracks, the World Bank

Track/ Level	Less senior ◄				► More senior
Technical Only	Assistant/ Associate	Young Professional/ Economist/ Specialist	Sr. Economist/ Specialist	Lead Economist/ Specialist	Sector Advisor	Vice President
Technical/ Managerial	n/a			Sector Leader/ Sector Manager	Sector Director/ Regional Director	n/a

SOURCE: AUTHOR

competition is stiff. In my case, for example, given that the total number of lead specialists in the education sector across all regions had a fixed limit, these positions were very competitive. Lead specialists, by the way, have a ranking equivalent to sector leader or manager. That is, both have the same level (and salary range) within the corporate hierarchy, even though the latter entails management responsibilities while the former remains squarely in the technical track.

The department sector leader is an especially interesting position because it cuts across sectors and countries (see table 3). For example, a Human Development sector leader is responsible for overseeing the work of the sectoral staff for a single subregion and reports to both the country directors *and* the sector directors. They therefore work closely with sector managers (for example, in the case of an HD sector leader, the sectors are education; health, nutrition, and population; social protection and jobs; and gender) and the country directors of their subregion (for example, in the Southern Cone subregion of LAC, this includes Argentina, Chile, Paraguay, and Uruguay).

Promotions were a complex process at the WB. As a staff member, you were expected to present your case for promotion, which involved, firstly, getting the support of your direct supervisor (sector manager or country director) to put forward your promotion case to the senior management team, preparing a thorough statement describing in detail your

Table 3: How Various Technical and Managerial Positions (Using HD and Education as Examples) Fit within the WB's Matrix

	Regional Vice Presidents, One for Each Region:						
Technical Vice Presidencies, Departments & Sectors	**Eastern & Southern Africa (ESA)** Country Directors, Country Representatives, Economists & Specialists	**Western & Central Africa (WCA)** Country Directors, Country Representatives, Economists & Specialists	**East Asia & the Pacific (EAP)** Country Directors, Country Representatives, Economists & Specialists	**Europe & Central Asia (ECA)** Country Directors, Country Representatives, Economists & Specialists	**Latin America & the Caribbean (LAC)** Country Directors, Country Representatives, Economists & Specialists	**Middle East & North Africa (MENA)** Country Directors, Country Representatives, Economists & Specialists	**Global Practice**
Human Development (HD) Vice President, HD Chief Economist	**ESA HD** Director, Sector Leaders, Chief Economist	**WCA HD** Director, Sector Leaders, Chief Economist	**EAP HD** Director, Sector Leaders, Chief Economist	**ECA HD** Director, Sector Leaders, Chief Economist	**LAC HD** Director, Sector Leaders, Chief Economist	**MENA HD** Director, Sector Leaders, Chief Economist	
Education	**ESA Education** Sector Manager, Specialists, Economists	**WCA Education** Sector Manager, Specialists, Economists	**EAP Education** Sector Manager, Specialists, Economists	**ECA Education** Sector Manager, Specialists, Economists	**LAC Education** Sector Manager, Specialists, Economists	**MENA Education** Sector Manager, Specialists, Economists	**Global Education** Director, Sector Manager, Specialists, Economists

key accomplishments since your last appointment or promotion, and compiling a list of reviewers at various levels of the corporate hierarchy and across regions and departments to provide feedback on your performance. These must be approved by your direct supervisor.

For each staff member's annual performance evaluation and promotion cases, the entire department's senior management team (which included the department's sector managers and sector leaders for the sector side of the matrix, and the sector leaders and country directors for the country side) would have a formal discussion. At some point, while I was part of the LAC region's education team, my colleagues and I joked that there were more people participating in the performance review discussions than there were actual staff being evaluated!

For example, within the Human Development Department, the senior management team included the HD Director, the HD Chief Economist, all three (or four) sector managers from the education, health, social protection and labor divisions, as well as all the HD sector leaders for each subregion. For the LAC region, there were a total of six HD sector leaders—one for each of the subregions, including Andean Countries, Brazil, the Caribbean, Central America, Colombia and Mexico, and the Southern Cone. Using the HD Department and education sectors as examples, table 3 summarizes how the various technical and managerial positions fit within the regions and sectors of the matrix.

Sometimes, Family Comes before Career

Axel, the country director who I worked with in the Southern Cone, was appointed to the same role, country director, for Colombia and Mexico, based in Mexico. He asked if I would be interested in a position based in Mexico City to work on education projects in Colombia and Mexico.

At the time of the offer, Tobias and Emilio were five and three years old, respectively, and the idea of moving to a Spanish-speaking country, where they could attend private schools and become fully fluent in Spanish, and where practically all our living costs would be covered by the World Bank, was *very* attractive. I discussed this opportunity with my then-husband, Charlie, who was in the midst of a competitive process to become head of an elite private school in Maryland.

We decided to prioritize his career for now, and I declined Axel's offer. Charlie too had entered as a YP and, at the time, was a senior education specialist working in the East Asia and Pacific (EAP) region. And, although he had previously taken leave from the WB to work in the US public education system a couple of times, he had been unwilling to definitively leave his WB international staff position. The prestige and compensation associated with working there were much higher than those of working as school principal in the US public education system, an option that he had previously seriously considered. This time, though, we both agreed that if he was offered the position of private school head, it would be a great opportunity not just for his own career but for our whole family. A nice benefit was that, as part of the compensation package, our boys would be able to attend the school at no cost to us.

After many weeks of interviews and meals with different school board members, we heard after Thanksgiving, in November 2007, that Charlie was not selected for the position.

During the 2007 December holidays, we revisited the idea of moving to Mexico as a family. We knew that the position that I had been offered had not yet been filled. I reached out to Axel and asked if he was still interested in me joining his team. To my surprise, he told me about an even higher position within the WB corporate ladder, that of HD Sector Leader for Colombia and Mexico, based in Mexico City. I would have to compete for this job, and it would lead to a promotion from Senior Education Economist to Lead Education Economist and Sector Leader.

Like many IDOs, the World Bank is generally a great employer. This is especially true for couples who both work at the same or different IDOs, as they want to ensure that the career options of married individuals are not negatively affected by those of their spouse. For example, the WB makes all possible efforts to accommodate a spouse's career when the other is being asked to move to a different country. When I was offered the sector leader position in Mexico, three directors—the HD Director for Asia, for whom Charlie was working at the time; the Global Director for Education; and Axel, the Country Director for Colombia and Mexico—agreed to offer Charlie the option of working from the Bank's office in Mexico City, as well as to work part-time for the EAP's education sector (since he was the team leader for Mongolia) and part-time for the Bank's Global Education Practice. This arrangement would allow him to reduce his travel to East Asia.

Before making such a big decision, we took advantage of a "relocation visit"—an all-expenses-paid trip to Mexico City to explore housing, schools, and the overall setup. The Bank provided a significant amount of support during our relocation visit. This included assistance from a preapproved real estate agent who showed us the typical neighborhoods where "expats" live, areas the Bank considered to be safe for families. We found a three-bedroom house that we thought would work well for our family. Also, Charlie discovered that the American School in Mexico City had several positions open—including school head, for which he applied and interviewed.

We came back home to Washington feeling excited about the opportunity to live and work in Mexico City for three years. The HD Sector Leader job was a great professional growth opportunity for me, and the boys would learn to read and write in both English and Spanish and become familiar with a culture that was similar to Venezuela's, where I grew up. Also, living outside of the United States would allow us to save significant amounts of money. We were so certain about the move that we even told the boys that we were relocating.

A few days later, as I was getting ready to travel to India as part of the Corporate Leadership Program, Charlie began reconsidering our family move to Mexico. After much deliberation, we notified Axel and the other two directors that, unexpectedly, we could not follow through with the move to Mexico City. Fortunately, all of them understood that I had very little control over this decision and the sudden change of plan, thus my future career prospects were not affected.

The next few months were some of the most difficult of my life, as I learned of some deeper issues that prevented Charlie from supporting the move to Mexico. As soon as the school year ended, I took Tobias and Emilio for a short trip to New York City. In his preschool class, Emilio had been learning about the Manhattan skyscrapers, and both boys were excited to visit them in person. I needed some time apart from Charlie to reflect on what was best for the boys and for myself given the circumstances. In New York City I decided to divorce Charlie. I concluded that my priority was to provide a stable and loving home environment for my young sons, and so, with that goal in mind, staying married to their father was not possible.

When One Door Closes, Another Opens

As my marriage was falling apart and having declined the promotion to HD Sector Leader based in Mexico, in 2008 I transferred to the global team of the education sector, now known as the Global Education Practice. Working for the Global Education Practice allowed me to limit the amount of time I spent traveling, as I would not be leading any loan or technical assistance projects. Instead, I focused on developing tools to better equip education team leaders with the evidence they needed to work on key education policy issues irrespective of their own background and training. Building on the comparative policy analysis skills I had gained while working alongside the government of Chile, I initiated a research project to compare teacher policies (including how teachers are recruited, trained, motivated, and paid, to how they are assigned to schools and the amount of time they are required to be teaching students) across the world with the aim of providing guidance to countries on what types of policies lead to improved student learning outcomes.

At this time, several of my colleagues were thinking about a project to "benchmark" education systems, and we began collaborating to exchange our ideas and approaches. Over time, our collaboration led to the emergence of the Systems Approach for Better Education Results (SABER) project. This was a flagship World Bank initiative to provide guidance to policymakers in the Bank's client countries on education policies to improve the learning outcomes of students. By 2012, the year I left the WB, SABER included modules not only on teacher policies, but also on early childhood development, public-private partnerships, education management systems, and school finance. SABER was being used by the WB's team leaders across all regions. Today, the Bank refers to the original project as "SABER 1.0," and it includes several initiatives that subsequently evolved from the original project, for example, SABER Service Delivery, Teach, and In-Service Teacher Training Survey

Instrument. According to the World Bank, SABER tools have since been applied in over a hundred countries across all regions of the world. In part, because of this work, in 2011 I was promoted to Lead Education Economist.

Yet, as 2012 would have been my fourth year in Global Practice, I began planning my next move. In February 2012, I received a phone call from the human resources department at the Inter-American Development Bank, inviting me to apply to be their next Education Division Chief. I had good friends who worked at the IDB, and I called some of them to learn more about the position. At the same time, I heard through the grapevine that two colleagues from the WB were also interested in the position, as well as the former Under-Secretary of Education of Chile, who had also become a good friend.

I recall a conversation I had with a close friend and WB colleague while I was considering whether to apply. I mentioned that a couple of good friends were applying, and that I wasn't sure I wanted to take part in a competitive process against them. My colleague explained to me that as our careers progressed, and there are fewer and fewer positions through which to move up the corporate ladder, it was inevitable that we would compete more and more with our close colleagues. He was right.

The IDB recruitment process for Education Division Chief took many months, and in the meantime, the equivalent position at the WB became available—Education Sector Manager in the LAC region. I applied to both positions. But deep down I knew that if I was offered the IDB job, I would leave the WB. The main reason for this was that while a WB Education Sector Manager is one of several sector managers across the regions, the position does not include decision-making authority with regard to project budgets. In contrast, the Education Division Chief at the IDB is the key decision-maker for all the Bank's work within the education sector—managing both people and project budgets. As I explained previously in chapter 5, "Navigating the Matrix," having access to funding decisions allows one to have an even greater impact. This was exactly what I was looking for—an opportunity to have an even greater impact on educational opportunity in LAC, as well as other developing regions.

The WB moved faster than the IDB in its selection process, and I soon learned that I was not offered the role of LAC Education Sector Manager. When the LAC HD Director shared this news with me, he also told me about another position for which he thought I was a better fit at this stage of my career—the HD Sector Leader for Central America. In terms of the corporate hierarchy, sector leaders and sector managers are at the same level. However, I was more interested in working in education than across all HD sectors.

I felt torn. I had not yet heard from the IDB, but I was pretty confident that I was not their first choice. My friend, the former Chilean undersecretary against whom (and others as well) I was competing for the IDB job, had many more years of experience and a similar academic background. It was only later that I learned she was in fact offered the job first, but that by then her husband was terminally ill and she had declined. In life's twists and turns, just as only a few years before I had chosen family over career and a colleague was instead appointed HD Sector Leader in Mexico, in this case my friend's family difficulties opened a new professional door for me. But I did not know this yet.

In the meantime, I applied, was offered, and accepted the position of HD Sector Leader for Central America for the World Bank. Although this position covered not only the education sector but also the health and social protection sectors—for which I had limited knowledge and experience—it allowed me to work in the LAC region again. This was now not only a professional preference but also a personal one, since it came with shorter travel distances and time differences from the United States. It was crucial for me to be able to minimize my time in the office so that I could be as present as possible for my two sons. As you might imagine, this is difficult to manage if you are having to coordinate calls with, and travel to, regions of the world in vastly different time zones.

I was going to move from the Education Global Practice back to the LAC region in June 2012, after a final mission to Australia, where we were to train technical staff from the country's international aid agency on SABER. However, the day before my trip to Australia, I received a call from the IDB's human resources department. The officer on the line asked if I was still interested in the position of Education Division Chief.

I explained that I was about to begin a new position at the WB, and I would only be interested if they could guarantee that they would make their final decision very soon. I did not want to be deep into a new job and depart abruptly. If they were able to decide quickly, it would be early enough that I could inform my supervisors in order to plan an orderly transition. The IDB officer confirmed that I was being invited to take part in the final step of the selection process—an interview with the Bank's president—and that the decision would be made immediately after the interview; I would be informed of their decision within a day or two after that final interview.

The trip to Australia, my first time in that part of the world, was a whirlwind. Flying to Brisbane took over twenty hours and I was there for only three days! I spent almost the same amount of time in the plane as I did in that beautiful country. The Global Education Sector Manager leading the mission managed to fit in a trip for all of us to visit a beautiful concert hall and hear the Brisbane Symphony Orchestra, as well as the zoo where we saw koala bears and kangaroos. Of course, we also spent much time training the Australian international development staff on our SABER tools.

I returned to Washington, DC, on a Friday, and the interview with the IDB president was scheduled for the following Monday afternoon. It would be my first day as HD Sector Leader for Central America for the World Bank, and I wasn't sure how I was going to pull off leaving the office early on my first day as sector leader to attend a job interview at the IDB! That evening, I received an email from my World Bank assistant. She explained that the office movers had made a mistake on my office move date, from the Global Practice to the LAC office, and that it was scheduled for Monday instead of that Friday. She asked, "Would you be able to work from home on Monday, while your move takes place?" Fate had once again intervened, this time on my behalf.

What lessons can you draw from my personal experiences about how to progress up the corporate ladder?

First, *take your time to figure out whether you really would like a managerial job*. Choosing to stay on the technical track will allow you to focus on applied research and operations. If that is what you love, do not feel pressured to switch to the technical-managerial track. You can be promoted up to a certain level (specifically, lead economist or specialist) without changing to the managerial track. If you do decide to pursue the managerial track, do it for the right reasons. I urge young professionals to avoid working hard merely to "rise through the ranks" as individuals, without having a clear impact strategy for the countries and contexts they are being paid to serve. While team leaders have a great deal of autonomy to schedule their missions and manage their agendas, as I explained in chapter 9 and will discuss in more detail in chapter 13, as a manager, most of your daily activities and travel schedules are determined by the needs of your team, supervisors, and clients. Being a manager can be a trying role at times and, unless you gain a great deal of satisfaction (like I did) from expanding your impact, you will become exhausted, frustrated, and unhappy.

Second, *don't take competition personally*. As you progress up the corporate ladder, you will be competing with your colleagues and friends for fewer vacancies. You will win some, and you will lose some. The good news is that while there are indeed fewer available positions higher up the ladder, there are many important and meaningful jobs within IDOs for every career stage, and the pay and benefits remain competitive across all roles. Many years later, I can confirm that I am still good friends with the former Under-Secretary of Education from Chile and other former colleagues who competed with me for the IDB Education Division Chief position!

Third, *consider the impact that a new job may have on your family, especially in the international arena*. I always sought out jobs that would allow me to have an impact and feel fulfilled while still being present to my children and family. As much as I could, I limited the time I spent traveling, which often meant taking overnight flights to and from missions in order to maximize my time at home. In some jobs, you have more control over your travel arrangements than others. Remember, children grow up faster than you think, and soon they'll be off to college and you'll be able to travel as much as you want.

Finally, *don't be afraid to take professional risks.* Throughout my eleven years at the WB, I spent most of my time learning and experiencing a sense of purpose each day. In other words, I was professionally fulfilled while holding a good, stable job. And yet, when the opportunity came to expand my impact on education in the LAC region—which is what I had been preparing to do for many years—I did not waver. I left an open-ended contract at the WB to join the IDB on a three-year fixed-term contract. Fortunately, my contract with the IDB was renewed three times, and I resigned at the beginning of the fourth. Had I stayed at either institution, I would not be where I am today. I was able to gain several insights across a broader set of IDOs through my work at Brookings. Now in my current roles as Harvard professor, director on several boards and advisory councils, occasional consultant to governments and nongovernmental organizations, and regular mentor to early career professionals, I find myself in a position of having even greater impact.

Part III

How to Make a Real Difference

11

Great Supervisors Attract Great People; Toxic Ones Push Them Out

It was in the fall of 2003 that, after graduating from the YPP, I joined the World Bank's LAC region's Human Development Department. At the time, having direct and speedy connectivity to the internet at home was very expensive, and thus few people had this luxury. I had heard through the grapevine that Ana-Maria Arriagada, the new HD Director at the time, was a working mom who strongly prioritized a healthy work-life balance. I think she was the first WB department director to have the department cover the costs of a home printer and internet connection for any staff member who wanted the option of being able to work from home. She explained that she did not expect staff to work extended hours, but rather that she wanted staff to have the flexibility to work from home, if necessary, given their parental or other responsibilities. I have explained in previous chapters why I preferred working in the LAC region; however, I want to emphasize the importance of knowing that the head of this department was actively supporting a healthy work-life balance—this was a critical factor in my decision-making.

I vividly remember the first time I knocked on Eduardo's, my LAC education sector manager, door to let him know that I was leaving early that afternoon to take one of my sons to an appointment. Eduardo, a proud *cartagenero* (i.e., from Cartagena, Colombia) who speaks a specific type of Spanish, filled with foul language and lots of humor, replied, "Why are you telling me this? Do you think I care where you are? You just get your work done, that's all I care about." His stance was incredibly refreshing at a time when I was committed to being both a present mother and a successful professional. I was immensely grateful.

Moreover, having so much flexibility to decide when and where to work (which was very rare back then, especially in large organizations) made my commitment to deliver even greater. I would leave the office religiously by 5:00 p.m., if not earlier, to get home in time to give my sons their bath, have dinner with them, and later supervise their music practice. Having been trained in classical piano during my childhood and adolescence years, music is an important part of my life. To my delight, the boys loved music too, and Suzuki strings became a regular activity in our home. After our practicing music together, we would go to my bedroom for book time. I strived to get them to bed by 7:30 p.m. After the boys went to bed, I would go up to my desk and work for another two or three hours. I learned early on that when employees feel that supervisors care about them, not just as workers but as whole human beings, they tend to work even harder.

One day, when I was still working as an education economist in the WB's LAC region, I received an email from the manager of the Bank's Global Education Practice. She was requesting detailed information on some of the education projects in the LAC region. I didn't know how to respond, as I was only leading a couple of projects in Chile and Uruguay and the rest of the projects in the region were led by other members of the team. I approached Eduardo and asked him for guidance. His response was, "Send that to me. That is bureaucratic crap, and that's what I'm here for. You're here to do the real work." As I look back, I am very grateful to him for taking on the internal bureaucratic tasks to allow me to focus on the work with the client countries.

I don't want to imply that Eduardo was the perfect manager—who is? He certainly had some unique quirks. I am not a fan of unnecessary meetings, but to build a shared sense of purpose and exchange valuable information, sometimes the most effective mechanism is to bring everyone together on a regular (if not too frequent) basis. Eduardo minimized the time spent in meetings to the point where his staff complained in a 360-performance evaluation (used to facilitate anonymous feedback to managers and other institutional leaders) that they never met as a team. In response, Eduardo organized his first all-staff meeting. But instead of coming prepared with a meaningful agenda, when we were all in the room, he asked, "So, you wanted to have staff meetings. What do you want to talk about?" The room was silent. That was the only staff meeting we had during his tenure as sector manager.

Yet, Eduardo, like most of my supervisors throughout my many years working in IDOs, established an enabling work environment that helped me, and my colleagues, thrive. Staff working under this kind of supervisor were able to enjoy ample professional autonomy and support leading to personal growth and project impact. Throughout my career, my best supervisors also promoted a healthy work-life balance. In the rest of this chapter, I discuss in detail some of the most important characteristics of effective supervisors. I also provide some insights into how to successfully navigate supervisors—at various levels within the corporate hierarchies—to maximize your impact.

The Best Supervisors Support Your Tough, Yet Necessary, Decisions

At the WB and the Inter-American Development Bank, many education projects included a school-infrastructure component. Yet, none of the staff members working in the education sector were trained as engineers or architects. They therefore did not possess the skills necessary to supervise the implementation of the school-infrastructure components.

I became the Education Division Chief at the IDB in September 2012, two years after a devastating earthquake had hit Haiti, affecting over three million people and causing immense losses for the poorest country in the Western Hemisphere. The IDB had stepped up to be the lead donor to help Haiti rebuild its education system, committing to providing $50 million in grants per year for five years, and raising from other donors an equivalent amount. In 2012, the IDB had already approved and granted the first two $50 million and was in the process of preparing the third grant for board approval. In addition, significant dollars had been raised from other donors, including the governments of Canada and Finland and several philanthropists. The Education Division team in coordination with the Haiti representation (the country-based team) had to oversee the government of Haiti's implementation of all these combined funds.

The infrastructure component of the grants to Haiti required all construction to be performed to a new stricter code to prevent the same degree of damage and destruction as happened in the 2010 earthquake from reoccurring in the future. One day, while still fresh on the job, I got a call from the IDB education specialist based in Haiti, who had just returned from a mission to supervise the building of schools. He reported, "I am no engineer, but I can tell you confidently that the schools are not being built to code." He shared pictures of pipes sticking out, cables falling from the ceiling, and cracks in the new walls of the very recently constructed buildings. The IDB had already discontinued contracts with some of the contractors who had failed to do any work; however, even the work that was progressing was now fraught with violations of basic infrastructure standards.

Of the $100 million that had already been granted by the IDB to Haiti, only $30 million had been used, or "executed"—the Bank's terminology. Meanwhile, my team was busy preparing the next annual Haiti education grant for another $50 million. This pulled staff away from time that needed to be spent supervising the implementation of the grants already approved.

I made two decisions that day. First, I would work hard internally to convince the country director that we should delay granting additional funds to Haiti until they were able to use them effectively. This is what is often called "low absorptive capacity" in development terminology. Even before the earthquake, Haiti had weak government institutions, filled with inefficient and often corrupt bureaucrats. The earthquake had completely destroyed the Ministry of Education's physical facilities and had significantly undermined the capacity of the government to implement the funded programs effectively.

Ending or interrupting an approved pipeline of projects puts a division chief in a comprised position, as it reduces your sector's relevance within the IDB strategy in a specific country. It is something of an ethical dilemma. If I had been more concerned about my own professional or financial advancement, and less committed to yielding a positive impact, I could have allowed the following three $50 million grants to move forward unquestioned. But it ran against my principles to throw good money after bad, and my values told me that it was irresponsible, almost immoral, to continue pouring money into Haiti given such low accountability and results for children's education. Fortunately, Santiago Levy, the IDB's VP for Sectors and Knowledge, a thoughtful economist who also cared about impact more than the size of the lending pipeline, supported my decision. Once again, a supervisor's role in backing me up proved critical to move forward in a way that would help ensure a better outcome.

The second decision I made was to partner with the Infrastructure Division, which had the engineers and architects we needed to help us adequately supervise the infrastructure components of the education projects in Haiti (and later in other countries). This type of cross-sectoral collaboration was unusual at the IDB, because it muddied the waters in terms of which division would receive credit for the project. I saw no other way to proceed and, importantly, it would also free up my team to focus on what I cared most about—getting students in school and learning. Fortunately, once again, Santiago stepped in and supported me.

This partnership between the Education and the Infrastructure Divisions was a real win-win. The infrastructure engineers, who usually worked on large-scale infrastructure projects such as building bridges and roads, loved being able to contribute to expanding educational opportunities for children and youth. One of them, a Chilean engineer who was about to retire, confessed to me that his role in helping oversee the school construction in Haiti was the most rewarding work of his entire IDB career! For the education specialists in my team, it was a relief to be able to focus on the teaching and learning components of the projects while knowing that infrastructure oversight was in very capable hands. This allowed them to focus on the educational outcomes we were striving for with this program.

There are at least three ways you can enhance the impact you're striving to achieve through IDOs. The first is to be able to bring the best, most recent, and most rigorous evidence of what works to inform the design and implementation of government policies and programs. The second is to build alliances within your organization and, as explained in more detail in chapter 8, "Globally Informed, Locally Driven," with your counterparts in the countries where you work. These local individuals understand much better than you all the political and contextual factors that will affect the chances of having a successful impact. The third is to, when given the chance, bring the best and brightest to work alongside you, whether you're the team leader of a project or the manager of a whole team.

The lesson from the Haiti education project reemphasized the importance of the TL's relationship with their immediate supervisor. Like my experience with other supportive supervisors, my team could not have achieved the targeted outcomes in Haiti without the support and encouragement to delay funding and bring in the appropriate engineering oversight.

As division chief at the IDB, I was often visited by "important" people passing through Washington, DC. In 2018, the then–Minister of Education of Guatemala came to my office to discuss how the IDB was supporting her efforts to improve access and quality of education in her country. She was a smart, committed policymaker, and one of her priorities was to promote inclusive education, especially of children with disabilities. As is customary in many countries, she arrived with a gift—a set of business cards with my name, title, and the IDB's logo that also included all the information in Braille. I expressed my gratitude and displayed them prominently in a business card holder in the center of the round table in my office.

A few days later, I met with my then-supervisor, the manager of the Social Sectors department (a level in the hierarchy above division chiefs, he oversaw the work of all the social sector divisions, including education, health and social protection, labor, and gender and inclusion). Later that afternoon, I noticed that the cardholder with the Braille business cards had been moved to the bottom of a shelf—essentially hidden. My assistant explained that the manager sent his assistant to ask her why I had these nonofficial cards and instructed her to stop displaying them. She did as she was told, but she couldn't help but tell me how petty she thought the whole situation was, from his not even asking me directly about the cards, and instead sending his assistant, to his ordering me to hide them. While I understood the policy issue around standard business cards, I was stunned and perplexed that the supervisor had not mentioned this concern when we met earlier. This was a different management approach from what I would have expected.

My advice to early and mid-career professionals striving to make an impact in IDOs? *Supervisors and mentors make all the difference.* For most of my career, I was extremely fortunate to have highly competent and considerate supervisors and mentors. In previous chapters, I describe the lessons I learned from my doctoral adviser, Dick Murnane, and my first supervisor at RTI, Luis Crouch. My WB mentor, Juan Prawda, generously shared his extensive knowledge of managing operations from his many years of experience, equipping me to lead projects and ensuring their continuity after his retirement.

Two days after my mother's passing, I received phone calls from Dick Murnane and Juan Carlos Navarro, my IDB supervisor, at my family home in Caracas. I am not sure how they found out about her death (I had neglected to call to let them know), yet I was very touched that they had reached out. Notably, they both told me to take the time I needed to be with family—that work, and school, could wait. Compassionate people like them make the best mentors and supervisors; they understand that everyone has a personal life outside of work and that we all will face personal difficulties and need to take time to heal. I have tried to model this throughout my own career managing people.

Eduardo not only allowed me autonomy in my work, but also gave me, and indeed everyone else under his supervision, the freedom not to worry about "punching the clock." Because he placed more value on the actual quality of my work, I was able to be a more present mother to my young boys and, in turn, this made me even more committed to my work and manager. Unlike many others who, once they have risen through the ranks, use their managerial power to delegate the bureaucratic work and not the substantive work, Eduardo went out of his way to relieve his team from the bureaucratic paper-pushing tasks that are typical of IDOs. He would take them on himself. Having had his turn doing substantive work as a team leader, he was at a stage in his career where he wanted the members of his team to develop their expertise in working with client countries. Further, Eduardo never hesitated to give credit when and where it was due.

Ron Smith, my manager in the WB's Global Education Practice, had many upstanding qualities. He was intelligent and kind, and allowed us a great deal of professional autonomy. At times, I think he gave us too much autonomy. While working under him, I learned that when intelligent, reasonable people disagree on how to tackle complex problems, there comes a need for a leader to make the final decision on how to move forward.

While developing SABER (Systems Approach to Better Education Project Results—described in chapter 8), my colleague, Harry Patrinos, and I had very different ideas about which methodological approaches to use when comparing and rating education policies. At the time, Harry was leading the public-private partnerships and school-based management modules, and our manager, Ron, held regular meetings with Harry, me, and our teams. In these meetings, we would present our best arguments in advocating for our preferred methodological approach. Both of us, along with our teams, were advancing the implementation of modules using our preferred approaches. The final products included rubrics, tools, and reports comparing diverse education policies across countries.

Ron, who could not decide which of the two proposed approaches the Bank should adopt, organized an all-day retreat with the entire WB education sector staff, as well as some external speakers. I vividly remember that summer day. My boys were on vacation with their father, and I was home alone. The night before the retreat, there was a severe thunderstorm, typical of DC summers, that led to an electricity blackout in my neighborhood. I woke up in the middle of the night to use the bathroom while it was pitch black. I hit my head on the corner of the bathroom door and felt blood running down my cheek. I didn't realize that I had slashed the skin and probably needed stitches. Since I couldn't see anything, I decided it was probably more dangerous to walk downstairs in complete darkness to get some ice than to try and go back to sleep while just using a wet towel to relieve the pain.

In the morning, the power had still not come back on. I was able to have a good shower and clean my face, but the scab and bruise on my face made it obvious that I had suffered a pretty bad injury. Perhaps even more noticeable than my cut was that I couldn't blow-dry and style my hair, which was, and still is, an important ritual of mine. My washed and wet hair went wild, curly, and frizzy as it dried due to the stifling humidity that is typical of summers in DC.

Despite my appearance that morning, there was no way I would even consider missing out on the all-day education retreat. I showed up to Ron's office early, before 8:00 a.m. The WB had a medical clinic at the headquarters, and I told him that I may be a few minutes late to the retreat, which was scheduled to start at 9:00 a.m., because I wanted to go to the clinic to get my wound examined. Ron, who was normally a reasonable and rational guy, glanced at the bit of dried blood on my face and said, "OK, but make sure you're on time." I was disappointed that he hadn't even asked about my injury, or whether I was experiencing any pain. I understood that he was under a lot of pressure to deliver a common approach for SABER, and that this retreat was the key milestone.

The retreat turned out to be a highly technical battle, primarily between Harry, myself, and our fellow team members. In the end, no decision was made—Ron didn't have the courage to choose a single consolidated approach and engage in a difficult conversation with Harry and/or me. For the remainder of the SABER project, each team leader adopted whichever method they preferred to compare and rate education policies across multiple countries. To this day, I still believe this inconsistency was a loss to the project as well as to the education team, which internally became more and more siloed.

Fortunately, the broader Education Practice was made up of relatively rational and diplomatic people, thus while we had strong differing technical perspectives, we continued to respect each other both professionally and personally during any weighted discussions. This experience taught me the value of engaging wholeheartedly in professional debates while, at the same time, maintaining healthy working relationships with one's colleagues regardless of short-term technical differences. Also, it highlighted that supervisors often have the final say in project design and quality.

Many years later, after I had left the IDB to join Brookings, Harry and I started collaborating once more. Since then, we have also coauthored several research papers about the impact of the COVID-19 pandemic on student learning across the world.

There may be other times when your direct supervisor is honorable, but lacking in strategy. In some cases, you may need to seek other allies to support your strategic decisions. For example, at the beginning of my tenure as IDB's Education Division Chief, Héctor Salazar, the Social Sector Manager, who was my direct supervisor, emphasized that although he had earned a PhD, he had long since lost his technical skills and had essentially become a full-fledged bureaucrat. He therefore enabled all four of us, the division chiefs for Education, Gender, Labor, and Social Protection, to make the technical decisions and budgetary allocations for each of our respective units. He was also generally supportive of our staff management decisions.

A few months into this new role at the IDB, I realized that to ensure a high standard of work that was translating into positive impact, I couldn't be the sole individual advising staff and reviewing analytical projects. I therefore introduced the concept of an "Education Support Team" (EST) and invited staff to express their interests in shouldering additional roles—beyond those of a regular team leader. These new roles included a lead economist, a lead operations adviser, and a regional coordinator—one for each of the IDB's subregions. Many staff expressed interest in taking on these support roles, and with the help of an executive coach that the IDB funded to help in my transition to the division chief position, we began delineating the various roles, responsibilities, and levels of accountability of the new EST.

One challenge I encountered was that there was no one in the team equipped with the training and experience to serve as lead economist in the way I had envisioned. We had a very capable economist on the team who initially took on the role; however, he was frustrated working alongside his fellow team members who did not have his analytical rigor. Instead of being willing to help them, he criticized their work. As you can imagine, this treatment was not received favorably by the rest of the team. Fortunately, I knew a respected and rigorous economist who had been living and working in Chile for many years, and with whom I had coauthored a few research papers. Not only did he care deeply about the quality of the research, but he was also concerned about how the research would impact policymaking. During one of my first missions to Chile as the IDB's Education Division Chief, I reached out to him and asked to meet for coffee, as I had always done before. I learned then that he was considering moving back to the United States (he was American) and was seeking interesting job opportunities.

I knew I had found my lead economist! I needed to make him an attractive offer (salaries in Chile were very competitive) to persuade him and his family to relocate to DC. I wasn't sure if Héctor, my direct supervisor, would understand the need for head-hunting a lead economist; however, I was fairly confident that Santiago Levy, the VP for Sectors and Knowledge (and thus my supervisor's supervisor), would be supportive. Up to then, the IDB had not invested in producing research on development challenges in Latin America and the Caribbean. Instead, most of the staff were focused on the Bank's loans and grant-making. Recently elected IDB president Luis Alberto Moreno, whom I met with in my interview, wanted to make the IDB a "knowledge institution"—one that provided not only financial resources to the region but also the necessary evidence to address poverty and inequality. To this end, the IDB was recruiting more and more PhD-trained staff, including the VP of Sectors and Knowledge (who had recruited me). He was leading the IDB's transformation from a primarily lending institution to one that also provided knowledge to client countries.

When I met with the IDB's VP to make my request, he immediately supported my plans. He also offered me an important piece of advice. He explained, "Now, call your manager and schedule a meeting between the three of us. I won't let him know that you came first to me, but I will be strongly supportive. You can count on that." Sometimes, you need to play politics; in this case, informally bypassing your immediate supervisor to gain support for strategic decisions. However, it is important to formally respect the institutional hierarchies. And so it was, by the end of the meeting, I had been authorized to install a new position for lead economist at a fairly high grade/salary level, and I invited the economist working in Chile to apply.

I learned that while having a kind supervisor is helpful, to have the most amount of impact, they also have to share your values.

In my final two years at the IDB, things changed and I encountered, for the first time in my career, a toxic work environment. A new manager was appointed to head the Social Sectors and would be my direct supervisor. He had been at the IDB for about thirty years. His entire world, including his wife and many close friends, were also employees of the IDB. He was politically astute and had risen through the ranks, primarily by catering to those above him. As he became more senior, he expected his subordinates to be similarly driven by politics and personal ambitions, and to treat him accordingly. This style of management, driven by control of information and politics rather than impact and purpose, was unfamiliar and foreign to me.

In 2018, I was invited to travel to Mexico City to participate in a regional meeting for the directors of education evaluation institutes across Latin America, hosted by Mexico's National Evaluation Institute. I was asked to give a presentation on global experiences with independent evaluation agencies. When my assistant and I were planning the mission to Mexico City, we realized that my presentation was at the same time as our weekly management meeting.

By then, my assistant knew that this manager would likely have an irrationally negative reaction if any of the division chiefs or the two advisers were late for or missed his weekly meeting. She advised me to write him an email to let him know ahead of time that I would not be able to attend the weekly meeting. I sent the email and quickly received a reply. He wrote, "I'd prefer that you attend the management meeting."

I knew that these were highly bureaucratic meetings, and I could not believe I was being asked to step out of a panel with key education authorities from across Latin America! None of my previous supervisors, not even when in my early twenties while at the Research Triangle Institute, had ever been "micromanagers." I also knew that after each weekly meeting, one of his advisers would send minutes to all participants, and therefore I would easily be able to follow up with any instructions later. Based on this, I decided not to reply to his message. After all, he had explicitly written the verb *prefer*, and I opted to take this literally. I assumed, or rather hoped, that I had some professional decision-making autonomy.

I skipped the meeting to make the presentation in Mexico. That evening, while back at our hotel, I received an email from his main adviser stating, "The manager will discuss the minutes from the meeting with you on your next one-on-one."

I was stunned. Unlike *all* previous weekly meetings, the advisers did not send out the meeting's minutes. I did not want to miss any information or instructions, so I decided to be proactive and called one of the advisers, who had become a trusted colleague of mine, and casually asked, "Rafa, was there anything important at the weekly meeting? Anything I should follow up on?" He replied, "Frankly, I was distracted because it was so very boring. But I think the key thing for you is that he wants the back-to-office reports to be turned in at most two days after you complete a mission. This applies to you since you're in Mexico finishing a mission."

On the flight back from Mexico to DC, I wrote the back-to-office report. I sent it via email as soon as I got home and had access to the internet. The next day, I was summoned to the manager's office. He was livid.

Ironically, during this period, the IDB's HR department was promoting "civility in the workplace," even holding an event with Christine Porath, Georgetown University professor and author of *Mastering Civility: A Manifesto for the Workplace*.[1] I attended the event and received a free copy of the book.

I reached out to the IDB ombudsperson—who in many IDOs is available to staff to provide confidential advice to address workplace conflict issues. She suggested that I share a copy of the book with my supervisor. She reasoned that his behavior was counter to what the IDB was promoting and that, maybe, if he read the book he would change.

Naively, I followed her advice.

The meeting with the manager did not go well. I tried to explain the impact that his behavior (micro and direct aggressions) was having on me and my team. I showed him the book and explained that uncivil workplaces can affect productivity and well-being. But, instead of showing interest in the book, he turned it over and said that *I* should be more civil.

I concluded that his aggressions were not only affecting my day-to-day work but also my ability to lead the team. And, as Porath points out in her book, uncivil workplaces not only affect productivity but, over time, can also affect one's health. I wanted to live a long, healthy life, and the stress that my direct supervisor was causing me was affecting my overall well-being.

Although I did not come to this decision lightly, after seven years as Education Division Chief, I knew it was time to leave the IDB. I did not want to leave the education sector, and no higher position at the IDB would allow me to continue working on education issues. To be fair, I knew when I moved from the World Bank to the IDB that should my time as Education Division Chief come to an end, I would need to move on, and that time had arrived. Luckily, I had remained connected with the broader global education and development fields, so it was not difficult for me to get an attractive job offer.

As you advance in your career, remember that *who* you work with and *how* you work are just as important as *what* you do. When you become a supervisor, remember to treat those who report to you in the ways that you would want to be treated. Allow professional autonomy and support to those who report to you. Be prepared to make decisions when it is necessary to move the work along. Great supervisors attract great people; toxic supervisors push them out.

12

The Power of a People Person

Hey, we all have a crazy aunt or uncle that we have to put up with only because they are in our family. Our team is like a family, but here we do have a choice. Let's avoid bringing in the crazies.

—Me

When I became co-director of the Brookings Institution's Center for Universal Education (CUE) in August 2019, one of my first activities was to meet individually with every fellow and staff member, a total of around twenty professionals.[1] During these meetings, I asked each of them about their professional goals. I also wanted to know what they liked about CUE, what they hoped would remain the same, and what needed to change. As far as possible, I scheduled these meetings over coffee or lunch.

Molly, one of the more senior research support staff members, was a bright young woman who had worked at CUE for at least three years. During our lunch meeting, she explained, "To me, 'Brookings' is the senior fellow and team that I work with on a daily basis. To tell you the truth, this is the first time that I've had lunch with another senior fellow." Indeed, each senior fellow managed their own research support teams, including research assistants like Molly, and as a result, these early career professionals seldom had the opportunity to interact with other senior scholars within CUE or across the larger institution.

From meeting with Molly and the other team members, I learned that fellows met regularly (monthly) with other fellows, and that research and administrative support staff met on a weekly basis to keep each other informed about the work. I discovered that there were no regular opportunities that brought fellows and support staff together. At the time, the CUE had about eight senior resident fellows, two of whom were co-directors, and another ten to twelve research support staff. It was not a particularly large team compared to the teams I had worked with at the World Bank and the Inter-American Development Bank. I set out to make some internal changes in order to build relationship bridges and communication channels across the different teams to explore potential synergies that could expand our impact, as well as to further enrich the general work experience for early career staff like Molly.

In previous chapters, I emphasized how important it is to have strong technical skills to get a foot in the door and make a difference working within IDOs. A doctoral degree indicates that you have invested a great deal of time in gaining certain skills, that you are someone who can persist and complete complex and taxing assignments—such as a doctoral dissertation. As IDB's Education Division Chief, when recruiting for an international staff position, if *all else is equal*—meaning all candidates have the same years of experience and similar backgrounds—and the only difference is that one candidate has a PhD and the other only a master's degree, I would always hire the PhD graduate over a master's graduate.

Having said that, the skills and backgrounds of candidates are almost never equal. Being able to relate to people of diverse backgrounds, work effectively with a variety of individuals, and be a generally pleasant person are all fundamental attributes if you want to succeed professionally in organizations like these. As I used to say to my fellow recruiting panelists, "Hey, we all have a crazy aunt or uncle that we have to put up with only because they are in our family. Our team is like a family, but here we do have a choice. Let's avoid bringing in the crazies."

Over the years working in IDOs, I learned how to harness the power of being a people person. You can have a much greater impact by making an asserted effort to work effectively with diverse personalities, as well as intentionally building and maintaining positive and productive teams.

There has been much written on emotional intelligence, and I can assure you it is an important skill.

What do I mean by "the power of being a people person," and how can you be one?

First, *understand your own tendencies and consider why they matter*. As a Young Professional at the World Bank, I participated in a one-week course for new team leaders. To prepare for the course, we were asked to take the Myers-Briggs personality test. I am agnostic about the accuracy of personality tests and their potential value for career guidance, but throughout my career, I have taken a few of them and find them generally informative. They give me insights into my preferences and leanings that in some cases have helped me address some blind spots.

In the case of the Myers-Briggs test at the WB, the course coaches analyzed all our test results and gave us individual feedback. In my case, I came out as a very strong extrovert, but for all the other categories, I leaned only slightly off-center. Each category has two extremes, for example, the opposite of E (extrovert) is I (introvert). They told us that each measure only indicates our preference and is not completely unchangeable; for example, although extroverts tend to feel energized by being around lots of people while introverts are energized by spending time alone or in small groups, there is a continuum between the extremes. Although I am very extroverted, I do still crave some alone time!

I mentioned earlier that I am also shy. I've learned that being shy and extroverted are not mutually exclusive. Similarly, many introverts I know are not shy. For example, in my roles as Education Division Chief at the IDB and co-director of CUE, I often had to represent the institutions at formal events, such as cocktail and dinner parties. On many occasions, I only knew a few of the other guests, and I found it awkward (especially being a woman) to introduce myself to the other guests, who more often than not were men. I would choose to stay with the few people I knew beforehand and, if that was not possible, find a way to exit early.

At the same time, once I feel I know someone and some basic level of trust has been established, I share freely what for many introverts can seem as deeply personal and private information. I love connecting deeply with others, and unless we know not just superficial details about our lives, that is unlikely to happen.

Going back to the Myers-Briggs, I placed closer to the middle in the other three measures and was assigned the ENTJ personality type. According to the coaches' explanation, the fact that I only placed in the extreme E for extrovert meant that I could work well with many personality types. In other words, I am a natural "people person." This resonated with my experience. It is easy for me to work collaboratively with many different personalities, and my friends also cover a wide range of different characters.

It also meant, however, that I can be *too* complacent at times. I like to please others, which has its drawbacks. I can sometimes ignore my own needs while focusing on those of others, and over time this may cause feelings of resentment. This had been a big challenge in my marriage to Charlie. After reading many psychology books and participating in many psychotherapy sessions, I concluded that he was a taker, and I was a giver. According to Wharton Professor of Psychology Adam Grant, "Takers have a distinctive signature: they like to get more than they give. They tilt reciprocity in their own favor, putting their own interests ahead of others' needs."[2] In contrast, Grant explains, "If you're a giver, you might use a different cost-benefit analysis: you help whenever the benefits to others exceed the personal costs. Alternatively, you might not think about the personal costs at all, helping others without expecting anything in return."[3] That imbalance, among other issues, led to our separation and divorce. Indeed, research suggests that in healthy marriages and friendships, most people act like givers.[4]

Adam Grant writes in his book *Give and Take* that in the workplace, few people act as pure givers or takers. Instead, he explains that professionals try to "match" giving with taking and coins this term "matchers." Whether you tend to give more than take or you seek the balance as matchers may, it is helpful to understand your tendencies as well as those of your colleagues, friends, and partners.

If you, like me, tend to brush off your own needs to please others, whether at work or at home, try to understand *why* you tend to conduct yourself this way. In my family, which was a more traditional upbringing,

I was taught that women don't show their anger but rather are always smiling and polite. To this day, when I get very angry, I would sooner cry in frustration than lose my temper. Some things are harder to change than others.

Yet, knowing my own tendencies has helped me, especially in later stages of my career, to draw some boundaries. For example, when I get an email with a request during the weekend, instead of feeling compelled to answer right away (unless it is an urgent issue), I force myself to wait until Monday morning to respond. In this way, I ensure to have the time I need for personal projects and activities, such as writing this book.

Second, *assume that others have good intentions, but be firm if you're proven wrong*. At work and in life, my rule of thumb is to always give someone the benefit of the doubt. In IDOs, you will work with people from many different cultural and disciplinary backgrounds. Do not judge your colleagues too harshly. For instance, US-trained economists, and others who, like me, studied economics though based in another discipline, are exposed to intense environments in their academic training, as professors can be quite aggressive in raising questions about the work of their students. Not surprisingly, economists can therefore become harsh critics of concept notes or other project documentation during the peer review process. Don't take critical feedback personally. I can attest that at least some economists can also be kind, fun, and thoughtful colleagues.

The reality, however, is that not everyone has good intentions. Once I have concluded that someone is consistently unwilling to be a team player, instead working only in pursuit of their own self-interest and agenda, I will avoid engaging with them where and whenever possible. That behavior is destructive to the culture I strive to create on my teams. It can be a catalyst to negative behavior in others, leading to reduced results and impact. I would never think of inviting someone that demonstrated these characteristics to join my team, even as a short-term consultant!

For example, in my first year after graduating from the YPP, I had two negative experiences with an economist who was only a couple years older than me. Our boss, Eduardo, the sector manager for education in the LAC region, had asked this economist and me to collaborate on a research project. Instead of treating me like a peer, he asked me to read several articles and books, and then draft a synthesis for him. I felt insulted—he was treating me like a research assistant, rather than someone with a completed doctoral degree a couple of years behind him. However, I continued to assume he had good intentions and, perhaps, was only unintentionally treating me as if I were his research assistant.

A few months later, the same economist served as a peer reviewer for a sector study led by another colleague, to which I had contributed a chapter analyzing trends in student achievement as measured by Argentina's national assessment system. During the peer review meeting, he referred to my analysis as "inaccurate and misleading," without providing any supporting evidence or reasoning.

I was stunned. With help from a summer intern, I had worked hard to analyze student assessment data from Argentina and draft a rigorous technical report. I knew by now how to analyze big datasets and make sense of statistical terms. I did not want to mislead policymakers, and I had no idea why this colleague was unfairly accusing me of doing so.

When Eduardo and the rest of the management team asked the economist, who was originally from India, what he meant by this serious accusation, he wrote an extensive email, detailing his deep knowledge of Argentina. He even included pictures of himself visiting schools and drinking maté (the traditional Argentinian tea) with teachers. He was trying to demonstrate that his contextual knowledge of Argentina was much greater than mine. Fortunately, it became clear to everyone that he actually felt threatened by me. He was hired as an international staff member after spending many years as a short-term consultant. As explained in chapter 4, this is not uncommon. As a YP, I had had a much shorter journey to my current position. His email reflected his own insecurities, rather than the true standard of my work.

In short, I realized that he was not someone with integrity and good intentions, and I have avoided working with him again throughout my career.

Third, *you should strive to work with people who are better than yourself.* As much as possible, you should surround yourself with honorable and well-intentioned colleagues. Aim to work for and with people who are more intelligent, knowledgeable, and skilled than you are. Never be afraid to work with someone who may "outshine" you. On the contrary, talented people who have genuinely good intentions will share their knowledge and skills for the greater good of the work, making *everyone* shine. As a team leader or manager, you'll be able to maximize the impact of your work by having the best and brightest employees helping to solve your project's most challenging development problems, *and* you will become a respected leader—recognized for supporting a highly effective team.

While working in the WB education sector's Global Practice, I had an interesting experience recruiting a junior consultant to work on a new project I was leading that compared teacher policies from various countries. She was already a WB consultant working for a different team leader. However, that project was coming to an end, and she was in search of new opportunities. She had also been recommended to me by Eduardo, my former manager in the LAC region, whom I respected very much.

During the interview, I asked her all the usual questions regarding her background, skills, and interests. I explained the goals of the project and the skills that were required. She appeared to be the perfect fit. Before bringing the interview to a close, I customarily asked the candidate whether she had any questions for me. She caught me off-guard, boldly responding, "So, Emiliana, what is it like to work with you?"

At first, I was a bit taken aback. No young person (she was in her late twenties, and a recent master's graduate) had ever asked me, their potential boss, what I was like to work with. Upon reflection, I considered her question to be a very smart move. I had already concluded from my interview with her that she had the right technical skills for the job, and now, I was realizing that she was also the right *person* for it. I knew by her bold question that I should hire her.

She turned out to be an outstanding consultant, who helped me produce some very high-quality research to inform teacher policy reforms. I went on to become one of her mentors—coaching her to get a PhD. She is now on tenure track at one of the top universities in California.

You may be forced to put up with difficult people in your family. However, if you have any influence over whom you work with or who to recruit to join your team, make sure to screen applicants for decency and kindness. When seriously considering hiring someone, I would reach out to as many individuals as I could to get a sense of how this person really was to work with. More often than not, those I consulted gave me candid answers, which helped me make an informed decision.

Fourth, *be kind and considerate.* I cannot emphasize enough how much more impactful you'll be when your colleagues know you're also warm and caring. Demonstrate to others that you genuinely care, not only about the work but also about the well-being of your teammates, supervisors, and administrative staff—make a deliberate effort to show them you value them as individuals.

Dick Murnane, my Harvard adviser and lifelong mentor, had a great practice. When he stopped by one of the desks of a university assistant to ask for administrative support, he always took out a small notebook which he kept in his pocket wherein he wrote the names of the assistant's children or something personal about them from a previous conversation. He would say something along the lines of "Oh, by the way, how is Emma doing? I remember the last time we talked she had a cold. Is she feeling better?" Dick knew that he wouldn't remember all the details of the many people with whom he interacted at Harvard, even though he genuinely cared about their well-being as individuals.

At the IDB, my job as division chief entailed making decisions related to our work assignments, as well as whether the staff would be based in HQ or in one of the client country offices. I did not take this responsibility lightly. I understood that moving countries not only affected the individual staff member, but often an entire family. In addition, some of the locations would be considered by many to be "hardship" postings, with their own living constraints. Factors such as levels of violence, climate, and altitude would have made the lives of certain individuals significantly more challenging. At the same time, I had to abide by the 3-5-7 rule (at least three years, on average five, and at most seven in a particular position), thus I couldn't allow a person to remain in a specific job (or location) for too long.

Figuring out my team's rotations became one of my most time-consuming and strategic tasks. I had to consider both the individual timing for each team member and the "domino effect": when I transferred someone to a new role, their previous job would open, and I would need to seek out a replacement. And then there were the political considerations, of which I became increasingly aware.

At least once a year, sometimes more, I scheduled one-on-one meetings with each staff member to talk about their professional goals and aspirations. I'd ask, "In which location would you most like to work next, and where would you least like to work?" This helped me get a sense of their individual preferences and inform what options I would propose to them for their next rotation.

Many people were involved in these placement decisions; it was not only up to me. A person who played a key role in these decisions was the country manager or director. I recall once proposing to transfer a staff member from Haiti to the Dominican Republic. He was a French national, married to an Ecuadorian, and they were both excited about the potential move. He met all the professional qualification requirements; however, when I told the country director about the plan, she vehemently opposed it. She explained that the Dominican government officials resented the IDB for moving staff from Haiti to the DR. I can only assume that this could stem from the long and tortuous history shared between those two neighboring countries. I would have to go back to the drawing board!

Obviously, all professionals have personal lives outside of their work. From the administrative assistant to the team of people you may be managing, always try to connect with the whole person. Learn about their families, interests, and general aspirations. *Word gets around*—your reputation as a kind and considerate employee or manager will spread and help attract the most talented people to work with you!

Fifth, *take risks and remain loyal to your values*. If you want to make a positive impact, you will need to take risks. Sometimes, you will require the other members of your team to take risks in order to get better project outcomes. There may be times when you need to confront government officials who may not be attending to their responsibilities as you would have hoped or initially agreed to. When things work out well, you will get the credit; however, make sure to always acknowledge the contributions of others publicly. Perhaps more importantly, when things do not turn out as you had hoped, make sure to take responsibility for the results, and protect those who have worked with you.

When I was leading the World Bank's operations in Uruguay, one of the project components included providing computers to all schools and transferring all primary school student records onto a digital platform. The purpose of this was to assist the central administration of public schools in accessing real-time data on student progress. I went on supervision missions at least twice each year to review the implementation progress of the entire project. During my first few missions, the report about this specific component said that it was delayed. I was told that the main problem was in Montevideo, the capital and where 50 percent of all the country's students attended school. These teachers reportedly stored student records in beautiful, leather-bound books and did not wish to switch to a digital tool.

I was a relatively new team leader and, at first, I believed this explanation. However, I'd always ask the project's information technology team to provide me with data, and after a few missions I realized that they were not being transparent. Finally, after many missions during which I was becoming increasingly persistent, they shared the school-by-school data with me. The data included which schools had begun using the digital platform and which schools were still resisting to do so. Immediately, I could see that Montevideo was *not* the problem. Rather, it was mainly a small number of rural and remote schools that were resisting moving data to the new digital platform.

During the debriefing meeting with Uruguay's Under-Secretary of Education, I mentioned that after a lot of digging, I learned that a few schools had not moved to the digital platform and asked for the government's help. The project director (my counterpart) offered an explanation by claiming that we needed to use project funds to buy new computers for all schools since the ones that had been purchased only a few years ago were obsolete. At this point I was frustrated, and for the first time in my career, I very firmly objected: "No, I will not approve this funding until all schools have moved the student data to the digital platform." The project director then clarified that the funding for the new computers would come from the government of Uruguay, and not the Bank. Every project has some amount of funding from the country's own government side to signal ownership and buy-in. This funding agreement is what is known as the pari passu. To access the funds for the procurement of new computers, all these government representatives required from me was a "non-objection." I firmly refused and the meeting ended abruptly.

A few years later, while I was with the IDB, I hosted a regional meeting of ministers of education. The former Uruguayan Under-Secretary of Primary Education, whose request I had objected to, was now the director of the National Public Education Administration. This position is the equivalent to a Minister of Education. On the sidelines of this regional meeting, she thanked me. She explained that because I had sorely embarrassed them during the debriefing meeting when I refused to give them the non-objection, Uruguay now had all their student records stored on the digital platform. Because of this, the National Public Education Administration was able to intervene as soon as a student began falling behind. This was certainly a nice validation that it was indeed worth taking the risk and standing up for what I thought was right!

Last, but not least, *nurture and share your networks*. One of the best things about IDOs is the access they provide to those who are passionate about improving the world in some way. You could spend your entire workday attending interesting meetings, presentations, brown bag lunches, and events discussing timely development issues. Of course, you also need to prioritize attending to your actual work. One thing I always made time for is networking. When you meet someone interesting, reach out and get to know them. You will build a network of colleagues, friends, and mentors to tap into for many years to come.

I have been very fortunate to meet outstanding professionals. They have spanned a broad cross section in my field, being senior, junior, peers, mentors, and supervisors. I have stayed in touch with my former professors from Duke, Harvard, and UCAB, my college in Venezuela, as well as my former colleagues from the WB, IDB, and Brookings. I consider many of them friends.

I jokingly told Dick Murnane that he did not know what he was getting into when he agreed to be my adviser. There is no important decision in my life that I've made without first getting his feedback—not only my professional decisions. When my children were young, Dick would always reach out while visiting Washington, DC, for a meeting or conference, and I would invite him for dinner. He would sit on the floor and play cards and board games with my two toddlers, later young boys. Over the years, they came to love him too. As young adults, my sons came to visit me in Cambridge and the four of us had brunch together, Dick getting a full update on their lives at college.

One of my research assistants, a student at HGSE, recently sent me a picture of a former colleague of mine from the World Bank, who had presented in one of his classes. The accompanying text read, "Amanda just gave a shout out to you for having given her her first job in early childhood development."

When I was in the Education Global Practice at the WB between 2008 and 2012, I came to HGSE to give a talk at an education conference. There, I met Amanda Devercelli, who was completing her master's degree. A few months later, she applied and was accepted for a position working for me at the WB. Together, we designed the framework to compare early childhood development policies across countries, as part of the Systems Approach for Education Results (SABER) global project. While I left the WB for the IDB only a year after hiring Amanda, she went on to have a spectacular career and is now the Bank's Global Advisor for ECD.

When I told Amanda that I was leaving, she said, "I'm sad that we won't be working together for long, but I'm glad that we can now be friends." We have indeed become close friends, and although she now lives in Kenya, we stay in touch as much as possible.

As I write this chapter, I am also working on a presentation that I will be delivering at the Vatican during the Assembly of the Latin American Business Council. Pope Francis will be there, along with the leaders of some of the largest industries in the region. My goal is to persuade them to invest more strategically in education programs where there is evidence that the programs improve student outcomes. I reached out to Luis, my supervisor from RTI, who is also originally from the Latin American region, and a very thoughtful person, to receive his feedback on the early versions of my presentation. His comments, as always, helped me improve the content of the presentation.

I hope these examples convince you of the value of nurturing and sharing your networks. Having moved several times across organizations, the mentors, colleagues, and friends I've made throughout the years have been an unwavering source of stability and support. I could not be where I am today without them.

The best part is that when, over many years, you work with smart, well-intentioned, passionate people who want to make a difference in the world, you will be in a position to have a greater impact yourself. At the same time, being able to achieve your professional goals while working alongside friends as colleagues makes for an even more fulfilling career.

13
Leading for Impact

Oh, now I understand. You're the classic middle manager.

—Rob Serraino

In 2013, for the first time in history, a Latin American was elected Pope. Luis Alberto Moreno, then the Inter-American Development Bank president, immediately reached out to Pope Francis to offer IDB support in the Latin American region. As it turned out, the Pope asked Moreno for the IDB to support the expansion of an education project that he had started in Buenos Aires, Argentina, while he was archbishop. President Moreno called my office early on a Wednesday morning in March to share the news with me, adding, "You're coming to the Vatican with me!" The trip was just a week later.

A few months before, I had started going to a personal weight trainer. I liked his method, "train until you fail," which involved using the weightlifting equipment with *just* the right amount of weight. Rob Serraino, the trainer, would keep detailed records of how much weight I was able to lift, and gradually added more weight. I was his first client for two mornings each week, arriving at 6:30 a.m. and heading back home by 6:50 a.m. Rob was an engineer by training, who built his own exercise machines and had a quirky personality.

I told Rob that I was going to have to miss our sessions the following week, because I had to travel unexpectedly for work. I didn't mention where exactly I was going. Rob, who never liked his clients to miss any training session, asked, "You're the chief, no? Why can't you control your travel schedule?" I answered, "You don't understand. My title is Chief of the Education Division, and I manage a team of thirty or so professionals and another twenty or so consultants. But I report to a sector manager, who reports to the vice president, who reports to the executive VP, who reports to the president of the Bank. And it is the Bank's president who is asking me to go on a mission next week. I don't really have a choice."

He then replied, "Oh, now I understand. You're the classic middle manager." He meant it as a joke, and we shared a laugh. But the truth is he was right. Regardless, I felt gratified being a middle manager, as it allowed me to have a greater influence on education issues than I had ever had before, even if it meant losing some control over my own schedule.

As I mentioned before, in the summer of 2012, I left the World Bank to join the IDB to become chief of their Education Division. In this "middle manager" role, I was responsible for overseeing a portfolio of loans to Latin American and Caribbean countries that amounted to US$3 billion per year, as well as an additional US$30 million in grants allocated to technical assistance. All funds were to be used to improve educational opportunities for the most marginalized children and youth in the region. Approximately half the team were working from the IDB's headquarters in Washington, DC, while the other half were based at IDB's offices located throughout the LAC region—from Mexico to Argentina and Chile. Perhaps even more important, in this role I was responsible for all personnel matters within the Education Division. This, I realized, was a critical lever to bring and develop impactful individuals as well as teams.

Although I had been managing smaller teams for the previous six years at the World Bank, this was the first time I would be managing an entire division. It was exciting as well as a bit daunting. Although I had thrived during my time at the WB, I had always hoped to be able to devote my career to improving education systems in Latin America, where I had undertaken the majority of my research and operations. I had witnessed how, at the WB, the expectation for all technical staff is that to advance in the corporate ladder, you must diversify more and more in terms of both the sectors and the regions in which you work. I knew I was leaving a terrific job that came with an open-ended contract, great pay, and added benefits. However, I also knew that if I did not take the risk to embark on something new, that would allow me to focus on *my* sector (education) and *my* region (Latin America and the Caribbean), I could regret it for the rest of my life.

My sons, Tobias (who in third grade adopted the nickname "Toby") and Emilio, were eleven and nine years old, respectively. I needed to share the news of my job transition with them but also to reassure them that it was a positive change. I remember the afternoon I picked them up from school in our Honda Odyssey minivan and told them that I was leaving the World Bank. They jointly asked, "Why?" I replied passionately, "Because I've landed my dream job."

I had been planning to work to improve my home country's education system since going to Duke University in 1991, and although my new job was not quite a position in Venezuela's government, it was as close as I could get.

It was indeed a big change. I joined the IDB's so-called senior management team and was tasked with managing people, assigning staff to work in different countries and specific projects, evaluating staff performance, and determining promotions and professional development opportunities, as well as curating an effective team. I had not been responsible for all of this before. Fortunately, I had benefited from a great deal of professional development opportunities at the WB. I had been primed to take on a senior management role, and I was able to tap into some of my prior leadership experience and the tools and materials I had been exposed to, as well as the knowledge and support from a network of professionals in a similar career stage as myself.

During this time, I read just about every book on managing teams that I came across. One common theme was that to establish an effective team, one must recruit the best people—or as I liked to say, *get the right people on the (school) bus*. This is much easier to do in the private sector, where most employees are at will, than in large bureaucratic IDOs where job security is extremely high and employees benefit from termed contracts for several years, or even open-ended contracts (comparable to academic tenure).

Another common piece of advice from the business-school books is to *be strategic with clear priorities*. I began wrapping up my eleven years at the World Bank to take on a three-year contract with the IDB. This seemed a risky move, as I went from having a stable, open-ended contract in a familiar institution to a fixed short-term contract in a new and somewhat different environment. I therefore made notes on what would be my key markers of success—ambitious but achievable goals that I could leave in place at the end of my first three-year contract.

During the period when, while still at the WB, I knew I would soon be leaving to join the IDB, I traveled to Australia to help train the Australian Aid Agency (AusAID) on our SABER tools. On the very long airplane journey back home, I worked on defining and documenting my strategic priorities. In case I were to leave the IDB after the three years of my first termed contract, I wanted to leave behind at least three legacy projects.

First, I wanted to develop a stronger team at the IDB than when I joined, where the effectiveness of our programs would be more important to us as staff than the size of the lending portfolio, which is a common marker of success (perhaps because it is easier to measure than impact) in development banks. Second, I wanted to establish a regional laboratory focused on promoting innovation in the Latin American education systems, as well as conducting credible research to provide governments and other institutions with valuable, independent data and evidence to enhance their decision-making. Third, I wanted to initiate a program designed to strengthen the professional capacity across the region's ministries of education.

While my IDB contract was renewed twice, each time for three years, I am proud that I was able to sow the seeds for all three of my legacy objectives during my first contract. The additional time I spent as IDB's Education Division Chief, four years for a total of seven, allowed me to make substantive progress on all fronts.

Building and Developing a Strong Team

On my second day in the job, Elena Arias Ortiz, an economist who was in her first YP rotation at the IDB, in a different division than education, showed up at my office. Before I had begun officially working at the IDB, she had booked a meeting with my assistant. As she walked into my new office, it was evident she was pregnant. She explained that she was looking for her second YP assignment and was deeply interested in working on education issues. She said she would be willing to work in my division after her maternity leave, even if I was not able to guarantee her a job after graduating from the YPP. She had done her homework and knew that I had no open positions. I told her that I needed a few days to think about it since it was only my second day on the job. I empathized with her, having navigated the YPP myself while raising a newborn and becoming pregnant with my second child. More importantly, she was clearly highly qualified, passionate, and energetic—all qualities that I look for when hiring.

In most IDOs, each department and division has a so-called head-count—a fixed number of staff. To recruit new people, someone has to leave. Yet, most IDO staff do not voluntarily choose to leave before they reach retirement age because the lifestyle, compensation, and benefits are all very attractive. When I joined the IDB's Education Division, I had no available positions to recruit new staff.

But I got lucky.

Shortly after my arrival, two senior staff, who by all accounts were below-average performers, requested to meet with me to ask if I'd support their departure from the IDB with a "package." People seldom leave before they reach the mandatory retirement date (which used to be sixty-two years but was recently extended to sixty-five) except for the few who are aware that they can negotiate a generous financial package if their supervisor wants them to leave. I wanted them to leave not only because they were poor performers, but also because with two positions open, I would be able to recruit new talent.

Fortunately, my manager agreed and supported the decision, which did come with financial implications for our sector, though not my division directly, to provide these two staff members a package (sometimes called a "bridge") so that they were able to retire with their full pension.

With these two vacancies, I was able to offer a longer-term contract to Elena, and I actively recruited a former consultant who had worked with me on SABER at the World Bank. Both women, who had PhDs from prestigious universities and relevant experience, elevated the quality of our team.

As I got to know my team better, I was better able to identify each one's strengths and growth opportunities. I became aware that there were a couple staff members who were underperforming, and I wasn't completely sure why. I decided I needed to do something about it, as building a strong team is not just about getting the right people in—sometimes you need to work on letting some people go. That can be harder than getting the right people in.

One of them, I'll call him Antonio, had been at the IDB for at least twenty years, yet he was not presently involved in any projects. He would come to the office each day, sit at his desk, and read books and newspapers, unrelated to work. I met with Antonio early on, and he explained that the previous division chief had "benched" him—or put him on the sidelines—and that he wanted another chance. I had done my own homework on Antonio by speaking with other colleagues, as well as my predecessor. The recurring theme was that none of his colleagues wanted to work with him. And that is why he had, in fact, been sidelined. Just like as a manager I didn't want to recruit people who are difficult to work with (no matter how bright they may be) to join our division, so do most professionals avoid working with difficult colleagues.

A few months into my new job, the IDB president asked me to organize a regional meeting of education authorities to share the US's experience with the model of community colleges. He believed that this was a good option for Latin American countries where the expansion of postsecondary education was too slow to meet the demands of an increasingly large share of secondary school graduates. Higher education was not my area of expertise, and I discovered that Antonio had worked previously on higher education reforms in several countries. I therefore asked him to prepare a concept note, a brief two- to three-page document laying out the key objectives for the regional meeting that I could share with the president to gain approval for the funding.

Antonio took about a month to produce the concept note, longer than I had expected. It opened with, "Ten years ago, the IDB held a regional meeting on the U.S.'s community college experience. Not much has changed since then." The rest of the concept note presented arguments against having the regional gathering that the president had requested. I couldn't discern an alternative proposal.

As the division chief, I realized I had two problems. One was what to do with Antonio. The second was what to do about the president's request. The latter was easier to solve, and I immediately found a solution in asking Elena to lead the preparation of a new concept note. After she delivered a splendid proposal and we secured the funding, she was responsible for leading the design and planning of the contents for the regional gathering.

Dealing with Antonio became a *very* time-consuming part of my job during my first three-year contract as IDB Education Division Chief. I first put him on a Performance Improvement Plan (PIP), and in close coordination with the HR and legal departments, I gave him work and carefully documented how he was failing to deliver as expected. This required weekly or biweekly meetings, which could often last longer than an hour. Furthermore, it was not easy to find work that was less urgent or important to allocate to Antonio. First, I had to secure the resources (usually from the country side of the matrix), which required making the case to a country director that the work was necessary and important for the IDB's goals in a specific country or region. Yet, assigning budgets to him was especially challenging, as he was likely not to use the resources efficiently and could put in peril the division's reputation internally, and even the IDB's reputation vis-à-vis the clients.

Somehow, after long discussions and a great deal of documentation throughout a little over a year, Antonio approached me to support him to leave the IDB with a package, which, of course, I was delighted to do.

I strived to demonstrate to the team members that I genuinely cared about them as individuals, while not compromising the high expectations I had of them. I recall one afternoon, when I had an especially long and difficult meeting with Antonio. A colleague, whose office was next to mine, heard when Antonio finally left my office and came by to say, "You know, many others have tried to do what you're trying to do. Not a good use of your time."

Indeed, while many of my colleagues assumed that getting rid of severely underperforming team members was impossible in an IDO such as the IDB, I managed to prove to them that there were ways to do it. More importantly, the difficult and time-consuming work of developing a PIP and documenting specific instances of poor performance greatly pays off in the long run.

Another instance where I was faced with confronting an underperforming team member involved John—the education specialist based in Panama described in chapter 8. After his contract in Panama, I managed to relocate him to Brazil, where I paired him with a very effective senior education specialist who I hoped could mentor him in operations. After a full year of close mentoring, John still was not performing well. I asked him to come spend a week at the IDB's headquarters in Washington, DC. There, I had a heart-to-heart conversation with him, during which he explained that he did not enjoy his work and that he really wanted to work more closely with disadvantaged youth.

The IDB partners with government and nongovernmental organizations to implement a variety of projects and programs—including projects designed to address issues faced by disadvantaged youth. However, until our conversation, John had not understood that the IDB's role was to provide resources and advice—*not* to actually implement the projects. A few months later, he shared some positive news with me—he had been accepted for a position at another IDO that functioned as an implementing agency, which we agreed was much better aligned with his interests. It was a reminder that talented individuals can find themselves in jobs that do not align with their passions. Successfully navigating toward a job that was a better fit for John was a win-win.

As I got to know each of my low-performing team members, I learned that some of them were indeed talented and collaborative, but they merely found themselves in a job that was the wrong fit. In such cases, if I could find another role that I thought they would excel at, I would offer it to them. I also learned to coach people out to a different institution, especially those who had lost enthusiasm to work in IDOs but were hesitant to lose their many financial benefits. Slowly but surely,

I was able to rejuvenate the team. As many of the management books had claimed, *having the right people makes all the difference.*

Making Ambitious Ideas Happen

While working in Chile, I witnessed the development with public funding of two research centers focused on education policy. Over the years of working in that country, I saw the tangible impact on education policies of the research produced by these centers. I was convinced that Latin American education systems would benefit from a similar regional center focused on providing research evidence to decision-makers in government. After securing initial funding from the IDB, I worked to make this a reality.

Like the World Bank, the IDB has a substantial amount of funding allocated to sectors (above and beyond the funds assigned for loans) through internally competitive processes. At the IDB, these are called Technical Cooperation funds. One factor that determines whether they are allocated to a project is for the project to have buy-in from one or more borrowing member countries. At the IDB, the most competitive, and also some of the largest, are the Regional Public Goods, from which sizable grants are allocated to fund projects that benefit at least three countries.

The first step to acquiring a grant to fund the regional center for Latin American education systems was to entice a team member to lead the preparation of the Regional Public Goods proposal. While formally I had the authority to assign these kinds of tasks, I firmly believed that unless the staff really care about the task or project at hand, they won't give it their all. I needed someone with sincere interest and passion to take this on. The person also needed to be strategic and detail-oriented, as I knew that the legal aspects of creating a new regional institution were not going to be simple. Fortunately, one of the most highly competent team members, Soledad Bos, agreed to shoulder this important responsibility.

Secondly, it was critical to gain internal support—including from the executive vice president and several executive directors, as well as those leading the Regional Public Goods fund. Soledad and I met with all the key stakeholders from the IDB several times during the yearlong proposal preparation process.

The third step was to acquire external letters of support from at least six ministers of education, and at least one from each of the IDB's subregions. Fortunately, half of our team was decentralized to the IDB offices based in the borrowing-member countries, and the majority of the specialists had strong ties with their respective government ministers. We managed to obtain letters of support from seven Ministries of Education, and the ministers presented a formal request for the IDB to finance the development of a new laboratory for education research and innovation. This resulted in a presentation at the Ministerial Meeting of the Organization of American States, held in December 2015 in Panama. Having many education ministers present the request at a high-level regional meeting went a long way to help us win the Regional Public Goods funding.

Today, at least seven years later, SUMMA, Laboratory of Education Research and Innovation for Latin America and the Caribbean, is an independent and self-sustaining institution that, without further IDB funding, conducts cutting-edge research and innovation to support education policymakers across Latin America.

Strengthening In-Country Capacity

Having worked for years on educational challenges in Latin America, I was keenly aware of how weak the capacities of the Ministries of Education are across the region. Yet almost every lending project I ever worked on at the World Bank, and supervised at the IDB, had a component to support "institutional capacity-building" activities.

During one of my first all-team meetings as the Education Division Chief at the IDB, I asked, "Raise your hand if you are leading a project that has an institutional capacity-building component." Practically everyone raised their hand. I then asked, "Raise your hand if the Ministry of Education with whom you work has the capacity to deliver results." No one raised their hand.

To change this situation, I asked the team to think about doing things differently. To help, I decided to allocate some of our own technical cooperation funds to develop a training course which we called "New Leaders for Education Systems in Latin America and the Caribbean." The course included the latest evidence of what had worked across the world to improve learning, with videos from key academics and policymakers discussing the central topics. The course also covered leadership skills training to promote the effective use of evidence by ministry officials, as well as other influential actors who didn't possess the same formal authority.

At the time, the IDB had just embarked on a partnership with edX, a free online learning platform that was created by Harvard and MIT. I was able to access an internal team of course developers at the IDB to help compile and design the lesson materials. We decided to offer an online course that was hybrid, including both synchronous and asynchronous lessons and activities, for cohorts of about forty staff working across the various Ministries of Education in the region. Our initial funding was used to develop the course content and to implement it across four cohorts—three for Spanish speakers and one for English speakers to reach the English-speaking Caribbean countries. We were able to secure an additional round of funding to develop a spin-off semiprivate online course for journalists,[1] as well as a Massive Open Online Course (MOOC) called What Works in Education: Evidence-Based Education Policies, which to this day is still running on the edX platform in both English and Spanish with tens of thousands of subscribers.[2]

During my first years as chief of the IDB's Education Division, I signaled to my team, both through words and my resource allocation decisions, that I prioritized the strengthening of capacity in the LAC region. I encouraged and empowered the teams to become actively involved in the process by participating in the development of SUMMA and the New Leaders course, as well as by rethinking the "institutional capacity strengthening" component of our ongoing projects.

Leaving with Impact

More recently, I met up with my friend Jishnu, who had started working at the World Bank at the same time as I did and is now a professor at

Georgetown University. I needed some advice, having decided to transition to academia, just as he had recently done.

As we walked around the Georgetown neighborhood in Washington, DC, he said, "You know, your team at the IDB is still producing rigorous research and is much more impactful in development than it ever was. You brought in great people." "Well," I responded, "I got really lucky. I had a great vice president who supported me, and I could bring in some great economists from the region." Jishnu laughed and replied, "Stop 'womansplaining'! Why can't you just take credit for what you accomplished, like any man would do?"

The truth is, at the IDB I learned the power of nurturing a strong team. I arrived with some strategic priorities and specific ideas about what I hoped to accomplish. However, what my team achieved—in SUMMA, the New Leaders course, and many other projects—far exceeded my initial expectations. By the end of my time at the IDB, my proudest accomplishment was that the team I left was far more competent and successful than the team I started with, and the impact in the region was much greater.

14

The Golden Handcuffs

When I stepped in to lead the World Bank's efforts to guide and support the Chilean education system reform, I did not have a clue how to go about it. I only knew that it was a crucial issue and once-in-a-lifetime window of opportunity that could fundamentally change the country's education system, and I desperately wanted to be involved.

Although I didn't have all the answers myself, I knew how to lead a team effectively, and I also had access to a network of relevant experts that I could recruit to join my team. Due to the confidence I had in my own leadership experiences and the expertise of the highly competent people I was able to consult with and bring on board, I was not intimidated by this challenging task. Reflecting upon my career, I have taken many risks professionally. My main motivation for this has always been the prospect of being able to make a greater difference in education across the world. Career-wise, it all turned out better than I could have ever imagined!

Perhaps the biggest professional risk I took was leaving the World Bank, where I was successfully climbing the corporate ladder, to join the Inter-American Development Bank—an institution that didn't have as many opportunities for growth and promotion beyond my position as Education Division Chief. Yet precisely because I was in such a high-profile position at the IDB, I was able to have even greater autonomy and influence, and subsequently new doors opened for me.

While I may have given up some job security when I moved to the IDB, I gained in compensation and benefits because becoming division chief was indeed a significant promotion. Later, however, when I moved from the IDB to Brookings, it came with a significant pay cut. Even though Brookings has a good compensation package as far as nonprofit organizations go, and my health insurance and pension savings plans were not all that different from what I had had at the IDB, my net salary at Brookings was 70 percent of what it had been at the IDB.

In contrast, some of my former colleagues who were passionate about improving education across the world while in their early thirties and forties have now been promoted to administrative and bureaucratic roles, or "pushing paper" merely to enforce procedures. I ran into one such ex-colleague recently at a conference. Like me, with a doctorate in education he had joined the World Bank out of a strong desire to improve educational opportunities for children and youth in developing countries.

However, instead of staying true to his passion, he advanced through the organization's hierarchy by taking on increasingly important roles. These promotions required him to leave the education sector, which was his area of expertise and interest, to become what I call a full-fledged "World Banker," someone who continues to move up the corporate ladder by specializing more and more in the WB internal policies and processes. After having occupied the position of country director, one of the highest-level positions on the country side of the matrix, he is now serving as a strategic adviser to one of the sector vice presidents at the WB. His position is now within one of those technical departments that I described in chapter 5, "Navigating the Matrix," where his main responsibilities include reviewing project documents that are all prepared by teams, and ensuring that they comply with the institution's policies and procedures. He admittedly hates these tasks and is looking forward to an early retirement with a comfortable pension. He is wearing what insiders call the "golden handcuffs."

I learned about these golden handcuffs very early on while I was being onboarded as a Young Professional at the World Bank. A human resources officer told me that she hated her job but would see it through because no other organization would offer her the benefits that she received at the WB. Truthfully, there was an older and *very* generous benefits package that was discontinued in 1997. I joined the WB in

2001, thus my pension and other benefits, while still generous, were not as attractive as those of my colleagues who had joined before 1998.

I must also confess that another reason I was more than willing to take professional risks is that having had my mother pass away in her early fifties instilled in me a deep appreciation for how short life is. I do not want to not to waste precious time working in a role or institution that is not well aligned with my own values and interests. As a result, when I find that I am no longer learning or finding joy and fulfillment in a specific job, something inside me screams that it is time to move on.

I would have left the IDB eventually—after all, there was no other position there that I would have preferred over that of Education Division Chief. However, my departure occurred sooner than I had anticipated due to the appointment of a new sector manager, who unlike the previous one and most of my previous supervisors, introduced a toxic work culture to the entire department (see chapter 11, "Great Supervisors Attract Great People; Toxic Ones Push Them Out"). I found myself unnecessarily and unproductively stressed about work. More importantly, some of the arbitrary decisions he was making were affecting not just me but my entire team.

I know that for people like me who come from countries where corrupt regimes have stolen power and ruined economies, the prospect of having to leave the United States and return to the home country or work elsewhere is extremely daunting. IDOs can provide a special kind of visa, the G-4, which is only available to international organizations' officials and waives the requirement to return to one's home country for those who, like me, were once on a J-1 (student visitor visa). I have had practically every visa in the US visa alphabet, from the F-1 visa as an international student during high school and my Duke years, to the H-1B visa while working at RTI, to the J-1 while studying at Harvard, to the G-4 at the WB and IDB, to the O-1 while employed by Brookings, and, finally, to my current status as a US resident! I can attest to how stressful it can be to depend on one's employer to be able to remain in the United States.

Financially, leaving a well-paying, stable position at an IDO may not be a realistic option. My friend who currently hates his job feels he cannot afford to leave his high-paying position at the World Bank given his current financial obligations and lifestyle. I'm sure many, as I do too, can relate to his situation. At the same time, there are many IDOs that also have good compensation packages, and it may even be worth considering a pay cut to land a more fulfilling job. That has been my practice.

While I knew when I decided to pursue a career in education that it would not be the most lucrative, I have been fortunate to have relatively high-paying jobs with generous benefits. This has provided me with the freedom to make healthier and more fulfilling personal and professional choices.

More importantly, because I didn't want compensation and benefits to dictate my career decisions, I needed to stay competitive outside IDOs. That is one of several reasons why I intentionally stayed connected to the field of academic research in education by publishing books and journal articles, as well as maintaining strong relationships with other academics and policy researchers. By maintaining these skills and the professional connections relevant to my field, I was able to avoid the "golden handcuffs."

What do I advise early and mid-career professionals who are already thriving in the world of IDOs?

First, *stay connected to the professional world outside the IDOs*. Whether you're a health specialist, an urban planner, or a transportation or energy expert, I recommend that you conduct empirical research and work alongside others to publish journal articles within your sector. Attend professional conferences as a means to establish and maintain relationships with other professionals. Stay up to date with the academic research literature within your specific area.

Work to remain relevant and connected to your field in order to keep your options outside of the IDO open. This will prove beneficial in the event that you decide to leave the IDO world. More importantly, this strategy will also serve to expand and improve the impact of your own work at an IDO. During my work on the project to advise the government of Chile or Uruguay, or when I was in the Global Education practice and had to travel across the globe, being able to call on a strong network of experts in the relevant fields, even if only to brainstorm, allowed me to bring the best global and local knowledge to my work.

Second, *unless you absolutely have to, do not stay in a job too long after you've learned all you can, or are beginning to feel unfulfilled.* Life is too short to not be learning, or to be wasting your talent. Once you've followed my first piece of advice, you will undoubtedly have networks to leverage when the time comes for a professional change.

Once I realized that my job at Brookings was not a suitable fit for me, I called several people in my network to explore other professional options. During one of my first calls with the dean of the Harvard Graduate School of Education, she asked me, "Would you be willing to move here?" I explained that my family had deep roots in Washington, DC, but that if she was open to me not living in Cambridge full-time, I would consider it.

A few months later, I had a formal appointment as a Professor of Practice at HGSE, and more than a year later, I am confident this was the right move. I feel excited every day I am in Cambridge, just like when I was a graduate student there. I love the diversity of the students and faculty with people coming from all around the globe, the stimulating intellectual environment, and the feeling that I am being professionally challenged in many new ways. I now spend my time continuing to do applied research on education challenges in LMICs, teaching courses to HGSE graduate students, doing university service work, participating in boards of interesting organizations that work to improve educational opportunities globally, and, of course, writing this book. To be honest, at times I want to pinch myself. I feel so honored to be where I am today.

15

Having It All: Balancing Family and Career

No way! With all these degrees and accolades, she must be single and childless.

—A CONFERENCE PARTICIPANT IN EL SALVADOR

IN 2004, DURING MY THIRD YEAR AT THE WORLD BANK, I WAS INVITED to a conference in El Salvador to present the findings from my ongoing research on teacher incentives in Latin America. The conference was organized by the Inter-American Dialogue, a nonprofit organization based in Washington, DC, that works to strengthen democratic values and economic and social prosperity across the Western Hemisphere. It was a valuable opportunity for me to get some early feedback on the key points that would be in my first book, *Incentives to Improve Teaching: Lessons from Latin America.*

The conference took place in a beautiful colonial-style hotel in downtown San Salvador, with redbrick roof tiles and dark wood doors and windows, which previously housed a private club. There were around seventy representatives from Ministries of Education across Central America, including the then–Minister of Education of El Salvador. At thirty-four years old, I was probably the youngest person in the conference. The meeting took place in a large, rectangular room, filled with round tables that could seat eight to ten each. At the front of the room was a podium with microphone and a big screen.

When it was my turn to present, the then–Director of Education at the Inter-American Dialogue introduced me, mentioning all my degrees and my title (back then) of World Bank Education Economist. I delivered my presentation, which was followed by a question-and-answer session with the participants. Afterward, I returned to my assigned table.

I don't recall if my cell phone lit up with a picture of my boys, or if I had another picture of them somewhere. But I vividly recall the comment from a forty-something woman seated at my table, who said, "Wait, you're married and have children? I was thinking to myself, 'No way! With all these degrees and accolades, she must be single and childless.'"

I laughed at her comment, but I knew firsthand how difficult it is for women to balance a career in international development with having a family. Especially for women who, like me, were raised in more traditional cultures. I have always felt that my career is secondary to being a mother and wife. And many of my career decisions, while turning out great in the long term, were taken keeping the family in mind as the first priority.

Today, when I speak to college or graduate students about my years at the World Bank and the Inter-American Development Bank, they can see the twinkle in my eye, the excitement coming through my face and words. Often, they ask, "Why did you decide to leave such an exciting career where you could have so much impact?"

There are many reasons, some of which I have already covered earlier in this book. The most important reason, though, is that, while I have worked hard to have a meaningful and impactful career, I have always strived to balance my career and family.

Ever since I can remember, I dreamed of having a loving husband and children, a big and supportive family. I can happily say that today I have all of this, and more.

But it didn't happen magically, or as I had originally hoped.

Throughout my time at the WB, I chose positions and supervisors that would allow me to have flexibility when I worked at the office or home (way before the COVID-19 pandemic made remote work common). I did most of my research and operations in Latin America and the Caribbean, not only because I love the region where I come from, but also because it is closer to the United States and in a similar time zone. Because I traveled mostly to LAC, my missions were most often less than one week long, and I could return home to be with Tobias and Emilio on weekends.

When my marriage to Charlie was falling apart, I chose to move to the WB's Education Global Practice primarily because I knew that by focusing on knowledge generation, I would not have to travel as much as in operational departments. I wanted to be present more than ever for the boys during this difficult time.

Being a working, divorced mother of two young children is not easy for anyone. But I was fortunate to be at an institution (the World Bank) with many job options at any given time and to find jobs with managers that, in general, were very supportive of work-life balance. Yet, I still remember when Ron, my direct supervisor in the Education Global Practice (or Human Development Network Education Department, HDNED, as it was called back in those days), said that I was "on the mommy track." I couldn't believe my ears; he implied that because I valued spending time with my family (and often minimized travel and hours at the office, as I explained in chapter 11, "Great Supervisors Attract Great People; Toxic Ones Push Them Out"), I was not as deserving of a promotion as others who put in longer hours. He was, of course, a white, American male—and yet, his wife was a full-time working mother of three, and I did not expect it from him at all. The truth is, all of us have our own unconscious biases, and he wasn't an exception.

Still, he supported my promotion from senior to lead education economist at the World Bank, and for that I am very grateful.

Later, as the IDB's Education Division Chief, I made it a point to leave the office by 5:00 p.m. most days, not just so that I could be home for dinner with my boys. I wanted to lead by example, letting those men and women who reported to me know that I encouraged them to balance work and family too.

In February 2011, a few months after my divorce was finalized, a close friend reached out. She asked if I was ready to meet someone. I had just started feeling lonely—especially on weekends when the boys went to their dad's house—and had just begun considering dating. She convinced me to go on a date with David, whom she described as intelligent, fun, and a good person. But what really convinced me to accept going on a blind date was that she said, "Listen, Emiliana, even if he's not the love of your life, you'll have a great evening—he's fun to talk with."

She was right that David is fun to talk with. But more than that, we quickly fell in love (though we took our time to tie the knot). After many years of dating and getting to know each other's children, close friends, and extended family, in 2017 we decided to get married and create a new, blended family. Our growing modern family is presently composed of David and me and our combined (adult) children: Charlotte and her wife Bethany, William and his wife Elizabeth, Henry, Tobias, and Emilio. And we have been recently blessed with two lovely grandchildren, Elliott and Trevor, Charlotte and Bethany's children.

Throughout my many years balancing a demanding and fulfilling career with being there for my family, I have learned that you can have it all, though not always at the same time.

The unpredictable schedule of the IDB Education Division Chief, where I often had to travel on a moment's notice, started to get in the way of spending quality time with David and our family. For example, David still remains very close to his college friends, and every few years they organize a reunion over a long weekend in interesting places. The friends usually travel for these reunions with their wives, and although we were not yet married, David wanted me to go with him for their 2015 reunion. I had agreed to go, assuring him that I would make every effort to take the time off from work. But then, a week before our planned getaway, the IDB president called and asked me to go to the Vatican with him to meet with Pope Francis. My now-husband likes to tell the story that after I had canceled many other trips on him due to work, how could he get mad when I put the Pope before him?

It makes for a good story, but it's also very true that it was hard to make firm plans to travel or spend time together. After our wedding, I felt it was even more important to be able to plan so that we could spend time together. And the appointment of a toxic supervisor helped me decide to leave the IDB. Thanks to my having pursued a different path while at the IDOs, and having stayed connected to the academic world, I had outside options.

As I write this book, Tobias and Emilio are in their final years of college. They are both stellar students and even better human beings. I could not be prouder of them, and I am thrilled that whenever possible, they choose to spend time with David, me, our large blended family, and each other. Most of all, I feel privileged to be able to work in a fulfilling job and enjoy time with my loved ones.

In my new position at the Harvard Graduate School of Education, I can take advantage of having a predictable academic year schedule and plan visits with our five children and their families, who live spread out across the United States. Equally important, I can continue to do impactful work not only through my work at Harvard, but also through many outside engagements with global organizations, as well as by advising governments and nongovernmental organizations. In fact, Harvard encourages all its faculty members to stay connected to the world through research and practice.

My advice as you pursue both a *fulfilling career in IDOs and a loving family?*

While there is no one perfect path that works equally for everyone, make professional and personal choices that align to your values and priorities. Base your professional decisions not on the specific characteristics of a job or institution, but on the potential impact you may have there if only for a limited time, and how that impact may open (or close) future opportunities.

My North Star throughout my career choices has been to expand my impact on educational opportunities in low- and middle-income countries. My positions in IDOs, think tanks, and academia have allowed me to achieve this goal through different platforms. In hindsight, each position has set me up for a new, more exciting one. But there is no way I could have planned the career I have ended up having from the beginning. As Steve Jobs so brilliantly put it in his commencement speech at Stanford University, "You can't connect the dots looking forward; you can only connect them looking backwards. So you have to trust that the dots will somehow connect in your future. You have to trust in something—your gut, destiny, life, karma, whatever. This approach has never let me down, and it has made all the difference in my life."[1]

I have seen many professionals too focused on work to be fully present when at home, missing out on real connections with their children and spouses. On the flip side, I have seen highly qualified professionals in IDOs (and elsewhere) who are not truly invested in having an impact through their work, and instead are holding a job to bring home the earnings to support a family. Yet, we all spend a healthy amount of our time at work, and if we don't invest this time purposefully, this takes a toll on our mental, and sometimes even physical, health. To successfully manage family and career, always choose to be present—at work and home.

16

Key Takeaways

Looking back on my career, I feel incredibly fortunate to have found meaningful and impactful work across think tanks, development banks, and academia. From a young age, I've been passionate to work to improve education opportunities in developing countries. This drive first led me to the World Bank where, like in other IDOs, I discovered the potential for tangible global impact. While the work, navigation of a complex bureaucracy, and cross-cultural collaboration were challenging, it was deeply rewarding to directly inform policies that benefited millions.

The power of education to change lives is immense, and I feel privileged to have been able to devote my career to this cause. At the center of this decades-long effort is my work to bring evidence to inform education policy in the so-called Global South, particularly in Latin America and the Caribbean. My heart lies in bringing evidence to the hands of in-country decision-makers. Providing them with the information they need to develop better policies, especially among those working to improve educational opportunities for children in low- and middle-income countries, has become my life mission. The time spent (more than twenty years) working in IDOs gave me a platform to pursue this mission.

And, while IDOs are by no means perfect organizations—for example, at times subjected to political interference and not always merit-based, just like most other organizations—they provide some of the best places for a passionate professional to have a tangible impact on reducing poverty and improving opportunity for individuals across the globe.

The good news is that there are many different IDOs in which you can help change the world for the better. From the United Nations and its many agencies to multilateral and bilateral development banks, think tanks, and consulting firms, there are numerous jobs and career paths for talented professionals. These include the Young Professionals Programs within many IDOs, fixed-term and open-ended staff positions, and short- and extended-term consultancies. If you are keen to work within IDOs, explore all of them as an entry point; it is common for professionals who start as short-term consultants to become extended-term consultants and also staff.

Depending on whether you want a global career or to work for your country of origin, you may pursue an international or a local staff position. Find a position where you will feel a sense of purpose and keep learning, and I am almost certain that new doors will open, as they did for me.

Many professionals within IDOs genuinely and deeply engage with difficult development challenges. However, often, there are more internal rewards for getting large projects approved and funding moved to countries than for conducting analytical work to inform policy. Thus, some become too focused on internal processes and rewards and, over time, get disconnected from their original field of expertise. I worked hard to stay connected to researchers and experts in economics and global education because, in spite of the internal rewards, I was always more fulfilled by generating evidence and advising policymakers than by getting an additional project approved by the board. This, in turn, allowed me to move from IDOs to think tanks and academia when I was ready to do so.

In fact, my career thus far has not come from an intentional plan. Although, of course, I had short- and medium-term plans and goals, at each important milestone I evaluated the options available with the goal of finding purpose, ensuring that I would be gratified most days by it, and ultimately to make the world a better place bit by bit.

For example, once I had made the decision to go to college in Venezuela, I chose to study my undergraduate degree in journalism because it provided the opportunity to inform society to make better choices and affect public policy. Also, I thought I would enjoy learning about a variety of subjects, including, among others, economics, history, sociology, and statistics. Similarly, after deciding to pursue a doctoral degree to deepen my knowledge of economics of education, I knew that I would not be competitive (given the lack of quantitative studies in my undergraduate studies) for a PhD in economics. I searched for alternatives and applied to the Harvard Graduate School of Education after learning that, once admitted, I could take any economics courses within the university. This combination of setting goals and having flexibility to pursue unforeseen opportunities has resulted in a more exciting, meaningful, and impactful career than I had ever imagined.

My positive outlook on life has helped me to overcome many difficult challenges. I firmly believe that if you do good, good things will happen to you. As my former WB colleague and friend Lant Pritchett put it, I've managed to get to and stay at "the top of the global education movement for a long time now," even though, or perhaps *because*, I've "always been nice." By the way, being nice does not mean being a pushover. I generally assume good intentions of others but, when proven wrong, I can be very firm. More importantly, I believe in the power of strong relationships to help you navigate a career with purpose and impact.

Perhaps one of the biggest challenges all professionals face, especially women who have been brought up in more traditional cultures, is how to balance an exciting and meaningful career with having a family. It was very important for me to get married and have children, and like most young women, I also faced the pressure of the biological clock, wanting to have all my children before turning thirty-five years old. This led me to make some not-so-great decisions, especially the choice of who to marry. Nevertheless, a priceless gift—my two amazing sons—came from this decision.

I was fortunate to continue to grow professionally, even after going through a painful divorce with two young children, and, later, to meet my wonderful husband, David Lawson, with whom to share the rest of my life. My two children, Tobias and Emilio, now in their early twenties, are smart, thoughtful, and caring young men. I've enjoyed being their mother every step of the way. My love for them is infinite and unconditional, and I could not be more proud of them. Indeed, my proudest accomplishment is our family. I feel privileged to be able to work in a fulfilling job and enjoy time with my loved ones. Having a stable and loving family life is a key catalyst for professional and personal fulfillment.

What could be more meaningful than contributing to improving the lives of children and people across the globe?

In my view, IDOs not only help to provide much-needed financial resources to low- and middle-income countries. Their most important role is giving decision-makers the information and evidence they need to make sound policy decisions. In the end, it is this technical advice that can turn the financial resources into sustainable investments with medium- and long-term impact.

Now from my role at Harvard, I am proud to be part of educating the next generation of education change-makers. I hope that by sharing both successes and failures, others may find purpose and community in this immensely rewarding field. With passion and perseverance, careers in international development offer countless opportunities to impact the world for good.

I hope this book has given those interested in pursuing careers in development the insights to *go for it* and to seek a purposeful career that makes a difference in the world.

Appendix

Appendix Table 1: The World Bank's Matrix (Only for Technical Sectors)

Vice Presidencies, Departments & Sectors	**Regional Vice Presidencies**						**Global Practice**
	Eastern & Southern Africa (ESA)	**Western & Central Africa (WCA)**	**East Asia & the Pacific (EAP)**	**Europe & Central Asia (ECA)**	**Latin America & the Caribbean (LAC)**	**Middle East & North Africa (MENA)**	
Human Development					*HD Sector Leader for Central America (~3 months)*		
Education					*Education Economist (~3 years), Senior Education Economist (~1 year)*	*YP 2nd Rotation (~9 months)*	*Senior Education Economist (~4.5 years), Lead Education Economist (~2.5 years)*
Health, Nutrition & Population							
Social Protection & Jobs							
Gender							
Sustainable Development							
Agriculture & Food							
Climate Change							

Environment, Natural Resources & Blue Economy							
Environmental & Social Framework Implementation							
Social Development							
Urban, Disaster Risk Management, Resilience & Land							
Water							
Equitable Growth, Finance & Institutions							
Macroeconomic Analysis & Policies							
Fiscal Policy							
Finance							
Trade							
Investment							
Competitiveness							
Poverty							
Governance							
Climate Economics							

(continued)

Appendix Table 1 *(continued)*

Vice Presidencies, Departments & Sectors	Regional Vice Presidencies						Global Practice
	Eastern & Southern Africa (ESA)	Western & Central Africa (WCA)	East Asia & the Pacific (EAP)	Europe & Central Asia (ECA)	Latin America & the Caribbean (LAC)	Middle East & North Africa (MENA)	
Infrastructure							
Digital Development							
Energy							
Extractive Industries							
Public-Private Partnerships							
Transport							
Development Economics							
Development Data	No regional teams						
Development Research							*YP 1st Rotation (~1 year)*
Global Indicators							
Impact Evaluation							

SOURCE: AUTHOR'S REPRESENTATION USING INFORMATION FROM THE WORLD BANK

Notes

Chapter 1

1. The institutions of the World Bank Group include the International Bank for Reconstruction and Development (IBRF) and the International Development Association (IDA), which operate jointly and are commonly referred to as the World Bank, as well as the International Finance Corporation (IFC), the Multilateral Investment Guarantee Agency (MIGA), and the International Centre for the Settlement of Investment Disputes (ICSID).

2. The United Nations' charter can be found online at www.un.org/en/about-us/un-charter/full-text.

3. Retrieved on September 10, 2023, from OAS's website: www.oas.org/en.

Chapter 4

1. "Nicholas Negroponte: The Vision behind One Laptop per Child," YouTube, January 16, 2007, www.youtube.com/watch?v=W5ySOqtxhbw.

Chapter 5

1. The WB's organizational chart can be found online here: https://thedocs.worldbank.org/en/doc/404071412346998230-0090022021/original/TheWorldBankGroupOrganizationalChartEnglish.pdf.

2. Email communication with Matt Brossard, July 31, 2023.

Chapter 6

1. The World Bank, *Bank Policy: Investment Project Financing*, December 1, 2021, https://ppfdocuments.azureedge.net/83f4ddea-a11e-4346-ab90-94ceb61ce03e.pdf.

2. Development banks also provide grants to LMICs, and these operate almost exactly like loans. The key difference is that in the former the countries do not have to pay back the funding, whereas in the latter they are contractually obligated to do so.

3. You can learn more about the Strategic Impact Evaluation Fund here: www.worldbank.org/en/programs/sief-trust-fund.

4. H. Patrinos and E. Vegas, "*Argentina: Building a Skilled Labor Force for Sustained and Equitable Economic Growth: Education, Training and Labor Markets in Argentina*," World Bank Report No. 31850-AR, May 5, 2006, http://documents.worldbank.org/curated/en/881741468202185592/Argentina-Building-a-skilled-labor-force-for-sustained-and-equitable-economic-growth-education-training-and-labor-markets-in-Argentina.

5. The national government's contribution is referred to as pari passu.

CHAPTER 7

1. Emiliana Vegas, *Incentives to Improve Teaching: Lessons from Latin America* (Washington, DC: World Bank, 2005), http://hdl.handle.net/10986/7265.

2. Emiliana Vegas and Jenny Petrow, *Raising Student Learning in Latin America: The Challenge for the 21st Century* (Washington, DC: World Bank, 2007), https://elibrary.worldbank.org/doi/abs/10.1596/978-0-8213-7082-7.

3. Sadly, Guillermo Perry passed away on September 27, 2019. Having served as Colombia's Minister of Mines and Energy as well as Minister of Finance and Public Credit before joining the World Bank, he was one of the most prominent economists in Latin America. More importantly, he was a kind, generous, and eternally curious person. It was my privilege to get to know him.

4. World Bank, *World Development Report 2018: Learning to Realize Education's Promise* (Washington, DC: World Bank, 2018), https://elibrary.worldbank.org/doi/abs/10.1596/978-1-4648-1096-1.

5. Emiliana Vegas and Lucrecia Santibáñez, *The Promise of Early Childhood Development in Latin America* (Washington, DC: World Bank, 2009), https://elibrary.worldbank.org/doi/abs/10.1596/978-0-8213-7759-8.

CHAPTER 8

1. Throughout this book, I mainly use actual individuals' real names. However, in some cases, especially when not shining a positive light, I employ pseudonyms instead.

2. Gringo is a commonly used term in Latin America to refer to American citizens, a Spanish-language adaptation of "green coats," worn by U.S. Army officers.

CHAPTER 11

1. Christine Porath, *Mastering Civility: A Manifesto for the Workplace* (New York: Grand Central Publishing, 2016).

CHAPTER 12

1. At Brookings, fellows are the so-called scholars, who are responsible for leading the research projects, whereas staff members tend to be early career professionals who serve in research support roles.

2. Adam M. Grant, *Give and Take: A Revolutionary Approach to Success* (New York: Penguin Publishing Group, 2013), Kindle, 4.

3. Grant, *Give and Take*, 5.

4. M. S. Clark and J. Mils, "The Difference between Communal and Exchange Relationships: What It Is and Is Not," *Personality & Social Psychology Bulletin* 19, no. 6 (1993): 684–91, https://journals.sagepub.com/doi/10.1177/0146167293196003.

Chapter 13

1. I had become convinced, and still am, that unless there is social demand for education reforms, they are very difficult to implement, as they are often too politically costly in the short run. Capable journalists can play an important role in informing society to generate such a demand.

2. See www.edx.org/learn/education/inter-american-development-bank-what-works-in-education-evidence-based-education-policies.

Chapter 15

1. Steve Jobs, Stanford University Commencement Speech, June 12, 2005, https://news.stanford.edu/2005/06/12/youve-got-find-love-jobs-says.

Bibliography

Clark, M. S., and J. Mils. "The Difference between Communal and Exchange Relationships: What It Is and Is Not." *Personality & Social Psychology Bulletin* 19, no. 6 (1993): 684–91. https://journals.sagepub.com/doi/10.1177/0146167293196003.

Frankl, Victor E. *Man in Search of Meaning.* 1st ed. Boston: Beacon Press, 2006.

Grant, Adam M. *Give and Take*. New York: Penguin Publishing Group, 2013. Kindle.

Jobs, Steve. Stanford University Commencement Speech, June 12, 2005. https://news.stanford.edu/2005/06/12/youve-got-find-love-jobs-says.

Patrinos, Harry A., and Emiliana Vegas. *Argentina: Building a Skilled Labor Force for Sustained and Equitable Economic Growth: Education, Training and Labor Markets in Argentina.* World Bank Report No. 31850-AR, May 5, 2006. http://documents.worldbank.org/curated/en/881741468202185592/Argentina-Building-a-skilled-labor-force-for-sustained-and-equitable-economic-growth-education-training-and-labor-markets-in-Argentina.

Pink, Daniel H. *Drive: The Surprising Truth About What Motivates Us.* New York: Riverhead Books, 2011.

Porath, Christine. *Mastering Civility: A Manifesto for the Workplace.* New York: Grand Central Publishing, 2016.

Smith, David J. "Free Yourself from the Golden Handcuffs for a More Purposeful Career." *Forbes*, November 4, 2020. https://www.forbes.com/sites/forbescoachescouncil/2020/11/04/free-yourself-from-the-golden-handcuffs-for-a-more-purposeful-career.

Vegas, Emiliana. *Incentives to Improve Teaching: Lessons from Latin America.* Washington, DC: World Bank, 2005. http://hdl.handle.net/10986/7265.

Vegas, Emiliana, and Jenny Petrow. *Raising Student Learning in Latin America: The Challenge for the 21st Century.* Washington, DC: World Bank, 2007. https://elibrary.worldbank.org/doi/abs/10.1596/978-0-8213-7082-7.

World Bank. *Bank Policy: Investment Project Financing.* December 1, 2021. https://ppfdocuments.azureedge.net/83f4ddea-a11e-4346-ab90-94ceb61ce03e.pdf.

———. *World Development Report 2018: Learning to Realize Education's Promise.* Washington, DC: World Bank, 2018. https://elibrary.worldbank.org/doi/abs/10.1596/978-1-4648-1096-1.

Index

About the Author

Dr. Emiliana Vegas is a professor of practice at the Harvard Graduate School of Education (HGSE). Her research and practice focus on improving educational opportunities in developing countries. She earned a doctor of education degree from HGSE, a master's of public policy degree from Duke University, and a bachelor's degree in communications from the Andres Bello Catholic University in Caracas, Venezuela.

Before returning to HGSE, Dr. Vegas was co-director of the Center for Universal Education at Brookings. Prior to Brookings, she was chief of the Education Division at the Inter-American Development Bank, where she oversaw the Bank's lending operations and technical assistance projects throughout Latin America and Caribbean countries. Before joining the IDB, she spent over ten years at the World Bank, where she led research and operations focused on education systems in various low- and middle-income countries.

Dr. Vegas has written extensively on issues affecting education systems in Latin America and the Caribbean and other developing regions. Her academic papers and books cover topics including policies to leverage technology to accelerate learning and skills development, raising teacher effectiveness, school finance policies, and early childhood development policies.

Born and raised in Caracas, Dr. Vegas enjoys spending time with her husband, W. David Lawson, and their large, blended family, including two sons, three stepchildren and their spouses, and two step-grandchildren. She enjoys boating, water sports, running, practicing yoga, traveling, and playing the piano.